Knowledge-Making from a Postgraduate Writers' Circle

STUDIES IN KNOWLEDGE PRODUCTION AND PARTICIPATION

Series Editors: **Mary Jane Curry,** *University of Rochester, USA* and **Theresa Lillis,** *The Open University, UK*

Questions about the relationships among language and other semiotic resources (such as image, film/video, sound) and knowledge production, participation and distribution are increasingly coming to the fore in the context of debates about globalisation, multilingualism and new technologies. Much of the existing work published on knowledge production has focused on formal academic/scientific knowledge; this knowledge is beginning to be produced and communicated via a much wider range of genres, mode and media including, for example, blogs, wikis and Twitter feeds, which have created new ways of producing and communicating knowledge, as well as opening up new ways of participating. Fast-moving shifts in these domains prompt the need for this series which aims to explore facets of knowledge production including: what is counted as knowledge, how it is recognised and rewarded and who has access to producing, distributing and using knowledge(s). One of the key aims of the series is to include work by scholars located outside the 'centre', and to include work written in innovative styles and formats.

All books in this series are externally peer-reviewed.

Full details of all the books in this series and of all our other publications can be found on http://www.multilingual-matters.com, or by writing to Multilingual Matters, St Nicholas House, 31–34 High Street, Bristol, BS1 2AW, UK.

Other books in the series

STUDIES IN KNOWLEDGE PRODUCTION AND PARTICIPATION: 6

Knowledge-Making from a Postgraduate Writers' Circle

A Southern Reflectory

Lucia Thesen

MULTILINGUAL MATTERS
Bristol • Jackson

DOI https://doi.org/10.21832/THESEN9605
Library of Congress Cataloging in Publication Data
A catalog record for this book is available from the Library of Congress.
Names: Thesen, Lucia, author.
Title: Knowledge-Making from a Postgraduate Writers' Circle: A Southern Reflectory/Lucia Thesen.
Description: Jackson, TN: Multilingual Matters, 2024. | Series: Studies in Knowledge Production and Participation: 6 | Includes bibliographical references and index. | Summary: "This book seeks to disrupt the narrative about the process of academic writing and the written products which are currently valued in the university. The author uses writing as both a subject and a method of enquiry in an ethnographic deep dive into her long-term engagement with a postgraduate writers' circle in an elite South African university"-- Provided by publisher.
Identifiers: LCCN 2023054863 (print) | LCCN 2023054864 (ebook) | ISBN 9781800419599 (paperback) | ISBN 9781800419605 (hardback) | ISBN 9781800419629 (epub) | ISBN 9781800419612 (pdf)
Subjects: LCSH: University of Cape Town--Graduate students--Intellectual life. | Academic writing--Study and teaching (Graduate)--South Africa. | Education, Higher--South Africa. | Group work in education--South Africa. | Authorship--Collaboration. | Learning and scholarship.
Classification: LCC LB2369 .T43 2024 (print) | LCC LB2369 (ebook) | DDC 808.020711--dc23
LC record available at https://lccn.loc.gov/2023054863
LC ebook record available at https://lccn.loc.gov/2023054864

British Library Cataloguing in Publication Data
A catalogue entry for this book is available from the British Library.

ISBN-13: 978-1-80041-960-5 (hbk)
ISBN-13: 978-1-80041-959-9 (pbk)

Multilingual Matters
UK: St Nicholas House, 31–34 High Street, Bristol, BS1 2AW, UK.
USA: Ingram, Jackson, TN, USA.

Website: https://www.multilingual-matters.com
Twitter: Multi_Ling_Mat
Facebook: https://www.facebook.com/multilingualmatters
Blog: https://www.channelviewpublications.wordpress.com

The policy of Multilingual Matters/Channel View Publications is to use papers that are natural, renewable and recyclable products, made from wood grown in sustainable forests. In the manufacturing process of our books, and to further support our policy, preference is given to printers that have FSC and PEFC Chain of Custody certification. The FSC and/or PEFC logos will appear on those books where full certification has been granted to the printer concerned.

Typeset by Techset Composition India(P) Ltd, Bangalore and Chennai, India.

The word reflectory in the title is borrowed from Clement Chihota's short story 'St Augustine' mentioned in Chapter 5, on page 88. The two main characters meet in a reflectory to explore time and space.

Contents

Figures

Acknowledgements

I am grateful to the National Research Foundation (NRF) in South Africa for funding received in support of this research.

It took a long time and many seasons to complete this work. It would not have been possible without contributions and conversations big and small along the way. Brenda Cooper's workshop and generous reading gave me impetus and inspiration. My deep thanks to Jim Petrie who gave this non-scientist courage to travel with surface tension beyond metaphor. Sharman Wickham talked me through an early draft with insight and patience. Thank you Sophie Oldfield, friend, neighbour and brilliant reader when I most needed it. Linda Cooper, Mastin Prinsloo, Viv Bozalek and Catherine Hutchings read generously. James Garraway, Sean Field and Vicki Igglesden, thanks for conversations and encouragement.

Warm thanks to the editorial team at Multilingual Matters. Theresa Lillis, most generous of series editors, thank you for the tough questions and support over many years. And to M.J. Curry and my external reviewer for reading with care.

When I lost my way, the wonderful people who criss-crossed the writers' circle always brought me back to what matters. Clement and Aditi, there would not have been a circle without you; and thanks to Ellen and Pippin for early days in the circle. Special thanks to Kim, Sibusiso and Teresa. Thank you to my inspiring colleagues at the Centre for Higher Education Development at the University of Cape Town for supporting this work.

To family, for support and help with design. Warmest thank you to Frances, Matthew, Andy and Max.

In memory of Brenda, Suellen, Moragh. And of Michael, who loved the idea of the writers' circle.

Note

Introduction: The Writers' Circle as a Portal to Knowledge-Making

> Agribusiness writing wants to drain the wetlands. Swamps, they
> used to be called, dank places where bugs multiply. As if by magic
> the disorder of the world will be straightened out.
>
> Michael Taussig (2015: 7) *The Corn Wolf*

Imagine a Group of Postgraduates

Imagine a group of postgraduate writers from different disciplines gathering every week to read and talk about each other's research. What would we hear? What could we see? Why does it matter? The multidisciplinary writers' circle that this book is about has been meeting regularly over many years at a university in South Africa. It has been a space where conversations, false starts, blushes, laughter, tears, hand-written comments on work-in-progress have usually, but not always, ended up as recognisable written products such as research proposals, theses and journal articles.

In my many years of association with the group, mainly as facilitator of the gathering on a Thursday afternoon but also at times as a writer participant, I have been captivated by the changing life of the circle. Sometimes the stuff left behind – the coffee cups, popcorn, lingering conversations, bits of paper – seems more alive and consequential than the written products themselves. The completed, archived theses and articles, rather than the scraps, appear to be by-products, cul-de-sacs from the entangled matter of a writing life. Within the circle and on its edges, writing comes alive, outside of the confines of the individual writing subject and the bounds of the discipline. Writing becomes profoundly social, challenging my thinking about how to support postgraduate students as they make their way as writers and knowledge-makers.

This book tries to interrupt the narrative about the relationship between the process of writing and the written products such as proposals, theses and journal articles that are valued in the university. The dominant narrative is that the process is only useful and interesting in service of a recognised product. I hope that both process and product may be re-imagined and that the stock image of the written product may be enlivened through greater respect for what an exploration of the messiness of the process can teach us, without the blinkers imposed by the product and its archives. I hope that the process of writing is seen not merely as a step towards a normative outcome, that it might become worthy of inquiry in its own right. In it are the seeds for imagining new possibilities for the relationship between writing and knowledge-making.

As teachers of academic writing, we tend to work backwards from written products after they have made their way into archives as search-able items in libraries and online portals and search engines. It is comfort-ing to find models of what we imagine an ideal completed text should look like. The written texts in the formal archive have recognisable genres, offering forms such as the PhD dissertation and research article described by John Swales (2004), that we can go to as mentors, as students who are learning to be researchers, and as teachers given responsibility to support students to access research literacy practices.

But these texts too easily come to stand for knowledge, shrouding all else. The influence of these pro forma texts that become blueprints for what knowledge looks like, is amplified by changes in higher education, most notably the shift to widen participation for historically excluded stu-dents (Wakeling & Kyriacou, 2010) in a sector that is increasingly shaped by market forces. The widening participation agenda emphasises the importance of making the practices of successful writers accessible to research students. Only the most privileged arrive at university with an identity predisposed to take up academic writing as a strength rather than a point of doubt and weakness.[1] Identifying a knowledge gap, marshalling the writing resources and the time, space, money and self-belief for this task require an immense effort. I argue that this work to become a researcher needs as much attention, if not more, than the written product, which is already stabilised and packaged in the problematic 'identify and induct' pedagogy (Lillis & Scott, 2007) that provides genre templates for the teaching of academic writing.

In the quest to embrace the powerful imaginary of the endpoint, we lose sight of what *might be possible*. While widening participation is on the one hand an attempt to democratise access to higher education, par-ticularly in South Africa where it has provided an important means of redress to the apartheid past, it is also a policy shift that expands the market of the knowledge economy with its global reach.

The problem of which genres have status in the formal archive and how to access them for knowledge-making becomes more urgent with the influence of the contemporary market-oriented university. This orienta-tion is obsessed with measurement (Ball, 2012; Peseta *et al.*, 2019) in service of human capital growth (Frick *et al.*, 2017). 'Knowledge' becomes a commodity that reinforces the notion of publishing as a form of currency that will accumulate citations and enhance rankings and reputations.

One of the ways the formal archive confers status in the academy is by seeing experience as unreliable. In what Stephen Ball (2012: 15) calls regimes of performativity that underpin the marketisation of research, 'experience is nothing, productivity is everything'. I have been aware of this problem of how formal genres occlude experience through decades of witnessing the struggles of both under- and postgraduate students as they work backwards from expensive, polished, written texts to insert themselves in academic conversations that feel alien. This deletion of experience has the consequence that for the aspirant knowledge-maker, particularly for students historically excluded from the academy, experience that becomes knowledge as it is filtered upstream in acceptable ways can feel like a betrayal of the richness of situated ways of knowing (Cooper, 2014). In Tim Ingold's (2007: 2) words, 'Life is lived along paths, not just in places [...] It is along these paths, too, that people grow into a knowledge of the world around them'.

There are many who are embracing the challenges of the times, resisting and re-thinking the logics of the marketisation of higher education and its expression in knowledge-making and writing. Moragh Paxton (2014) for example focuses on the genre of the research proposal as a contested site, offering creative ways for writing teachers and supervisors to engage with the prior experience of postgraduate scholars from a range of professional backgrounds. Her chapter challenges the way writing specialists become 'purveyors of genre' (2014: 164) as settled forms.

The emphasis in this book is on the entanglements of the processual life of the Thursday writers' circle in an historically privileged post-apartheid Southern African university, the University of Cape Town (UCT), set within the far-reaching broader societal shifts in global higher education. Seen through the market-driven lens of efficiency and time-is-money, the stuff along the way is shed, sloughed off as waste-matter, as collateral, an inevitable culling to arrive at something deemed to be worthy of postgraduate certification or publication. But it is also the stuff of joy, generosity and hopes sometimes gone wrong, of misdirected efforts, compromises and often of shame. I focus more on this extra-textual life – the affect, materialities, presence and absence, refusals and moments of yielding – than on evolving textual histories that are gradually given shape over time before arriving at completion of a product-for-now. This study comes in alongside work on critical approaches to text trajectories (Blommaert, 2005; Lillis & Maybin, 2017) and the textual histories of theses and journal articles (Canagarajah & Lee, 2014; Casanave, 2010; Casanave & Vandrick, 2003; Lillis & Curry, 2010) but from a different angle. There is no assumed directionality: it begins in the middle, working from the circle as a loosely held, almost *ad hoc* pedagogic space that is as confusing as it is energising. The stuff that is left behind leaves a trace, a residue of memory, happenings, feelings, things done and undone, that is consequential. Ghosts from this residue haunt the corridors of the formal archive and its imaginaries.

Traces and Archives

It is this residual material that interests Geoffrey Bowker (2010) in what he calls the trace archive – the unofficial, often anecdotal, subaltern pathways of informal practice that are in the shadow of formal scientific practice and method, shaped by contemporary technologies. While this trace-work happens everywhere, in laboratories and libraries as well as spaces that resist the formal archive or are alienated from it, Bowker brackets it conceptually as an archive in a move to challenge and expand the formal or 'jussive' archive (following Derrida, 1996), which domesticates and gives instructions for conduct. By seeming to conserve and authorise, the jussive force 'operates through being invisibly exclusionary' (Bowker, 2005: 14). Achille Mbembe (2002) puts it well: 'the inescapable materiality of the archive [...] does away with doubt' (2002: 21). It is:

> fundamentally a matter of discrimination and selection, which, in the end results in the granting of a privileged status to certain written documents, and a refusal of that same status to others, thereby judged 'unarchivable'. The archive is therefore, not a piece of data, but a status. (2002: 20)

The term trace can help us to understand how the formal archive eliminates doubt. Trace is more than experience, and more than the spoor left behind lives lived along paths, like the popcorn and empty teacups and fragments of languaging in the wake of the circle. It does additional work for Jacques Derrida in his earlier writing on language (1976) and Judith Butler (1990, 1993) and others who emphasise the function of language as performance rather than language as representation or competence. Seen as performance, language is constitutive, which includes the function of making distinctions. We derive meaning from signs because they are different from other signs. By giving something a name, we are saying it is this, not that. Knowledge not ignorance; light not dark; man not woman. But what is excluded in naming practices 'doesn't quite go away' (Butler, 1993, in Prinsloo, 2022: 92). This exclusion becomes potent when signs are used in binary pairs: through routine and repetition, a distinction is implied, even if it is unsaid. And a judgment is enacted. Because binary terms are contingent, the excluded term functions as a kind of haunting. It is present in its absence. The favoured, sanctioned term, such as 'knowledge' or 'western' piggybacks on its other, which is suppressed but still potent. This 'not quite going away' is where the trace lives.

My use of the term trace moves about in the book. I use the term trace archive to signal a status rather than a collection of data, and the trace, trace-making and trace-work to denote activities that go on within this unauthorised, seemingly low-stakes, swampy space. This is not to be confused with Gilles Deleuze and Felix Guattari's (1987: 13) notion of tracing as a reproduction: 'like a photograph or X ray that begins by selecting or isolating, by artificial means such as colorations or other restrictive procedures, what it intends to reproduce'. Their notion of trace and tracing relates to the activity of using tracing paper to represent and copy faithfully the relationship between elements that constitute a representation of a scene of interest. In contrast my use of trace is interested in a quest to honour the ephemeral, discarded, sensed but not seen aspects of knowledge-making, to keep them in motion rather than to capture them.

The idea of the formal archive as a status bolstered by the materiality that has accrued around an ideology of 'writtenness' (Turner, 2018) is an important motivation for this book. Attending to the trace archive requires working differently. Unlike the formal archive which is bounded, lending itself to classification and counting, the trace archive is largely freewheeling and intuitive, about duration and wayfaring. It is difficult to pin down to time and place. Searching and finding the trace most often involves going against the grain, outside of the library, the internet and easy-to-access knowledges that come commodified and packaged.

I foreground the trace in order to keep it in conversation with its other, the formal archive. Like Bowker (2010), I am working towards an expanded notion of the archive as 'the set of all events that can be recalled across time and space' (2010: 212). Foregrounding the trace and the trace archive to widen and deepen what counts as knowledge needs work that is less shaped by disciplinary knowledges and methodological orthodoxies than by affect. Affect is understood as embodied feel for how to act and interact with a range of others (human and non-human, real and imagined) in the process of becoming (Massumi, 1987). This commitment to go where something's happening can be done with the help of modes of inquiry that thrive on memory, narrative, anecdote, synchronicity and vulnerability to explore affective potentials with an eye on future possibilities.

Exploring Interfaces: Surface Tension

Surface tension is an important idea in my quest to explore what is happening at the interface between formal and informal archives. Early in this inquiry it appealed to me intuitively as a way of thinking about academic writing: writing is material in that it covers surfaces such as paper, screen and empty pages that are incrementally filled one word at a time. Arranging the words in a particular order in a named language (increasingly English) so that one may be understood by high-stakes readers is to say the least filled with tensions of many kinds as the writer negotiates the struggle between inner and outer worlds.

I adopt and adapt the concept of surface tension from the physical sciences and travel with it. Surface tension is an integral part of the physical sciences. It plays out across different scales, and influences everything from the selection of materials to all situations where interfaces and their interactions are relevant. It is a relational idea that works in the space between (at least) two entities in contact. The edge between entities is alive and not always easy to hold still. Think of when air meets water as in the formation of bubbles or drops of water on a leaf as heterogenous entities interact.

Instead of seeing interfaces as in a vertical relationship, I imagine elements as flattened on the horizontal plane, next to each other. Although the formal archive yearns for it, there is no clear once-and-for-all hierarchical divide between trace and formal archives. The word product conjures up the term process as binary opposite. In the circle, there is no hierarchical divide between process and product. Product is not 'better' than process; formal genres do not trump experience. The Thursday writers' circle is one of the spaces where the trace emerges, calling out the distinction between official and unofficial, process and product, depth and surface. In this book I try to pause this moment of emergence by invoking the circle as a portal – a bi-directional gateway breeching the formal archive. The circle is less a place than a contact zone of entangled relations 'where there are no insiders and outsiders, only openings and ways through' (Ingold, 2007: 103).

In seeing the two archives as next to each rather – proximate rather than in a relationship of hierarchy – I am also questioning the way we juxtapose surface and depth in teaching and learning. Another binary pair: surface is understood as superficial, in some kind of moral opposition to depth. This plays out in the distinction between surface and deep learning that has been so influential in higher education studies (Biggs & Tang, 2007; Entwistle & Ramsden, 1983; Marton & Saljo, 1976). Surface is seen as rote learning, involving memorisation, while deep learning is understood as a display of integration and investment in meaning. Surface is weak; deep is rich and full. The narrative is that 'struggling' students are in deficit and should be taken from surface learning to a deep approach, creating a logic that is 'another valorisation of the western Enlightenment' (Howie & Bagnall, 2013). In a similar way, the imaginary of the formal archive contributes to the sense of alienation experienced by many postgraduate scholars.

So surface tension is a concept-at-work across this book, a way of exploring interfaces without resolving them. It is an *idea in action,* at play across the chapters, strongly present in some, particularly in Chapter 3, 'Surface Tension: Writing in the Shadow of the God View', while only suggested in others. It informs how I explore other interfaces besides formal (largely conventional, written) and informal (experiential) archives. It is there in the interface between subjective and objective in writing and between self and other more widely as I hope to expand the idea of knowledge beyond the conventional, cleaned up written texts that occupy the archive as an imaginary – a status that dismisses doubt.

The Turbulent Archive(s) of Writing in the South

I come to my interest in how the writers' circle can open portals to knowledge-making via immersion in the field of Academic Literacies (Lea & Street, 1998; Lillis & Scott, 2007). As a burgeoning field of scholarship and practice, it too has sub-archives that are settling into patterns of attribution and at the same time alive and swirling with currents. It is as close to a disciplinary home as I have found. It foregrounds literacy as situated social practice but with an insistence that this be understood through a critical lens as a counter to prevailing ideologies that see student deficit everywhere. In deficit approaches 'the emphasis tends to be overwhelmingly on what student writers don't or can't do in academic writing, rather than on what they can, or would like to' achieve in their writing (Lillis *et al.*, 2015: 5).

Academic Literacies is a hybrid, given impetus by the widening participation policy agenda. In the UK and South Africa[2] in particular, this hybrid aims to counter deficit notions of students through social practice understandings of academic writing. It gained impetus from work under way in the New Literacy Studies (Gee, 1990; Prinsloo & Breier, 1996; Street, 1984). Academic Literacies is also a conversation within the study of language more broadly, specifically Applied Linguistics, though I prefer the version named as Applied Language Studies, as it draws attention to a collection of elements gathered for a particular task, rather than as aligned with the discipline of Linguistics. I like Alistair Pennycook's (2018: 129) notion of epistemic assemblage: 'temporary assemblage of thought and action that come together at particular moments when language-related concerns need to be addressed'. In this book, I make an epistemic assemblage from where I am in the global south, inescapably speaking with a southern accent that is a jumbled confluence of different postcolonial currents, with the urgencies and contradictions of working in an elite university in the global south.

The global drivers of the marketisation of higher education and widening access play out in particular and often contradictory ways across South African higher education. This university, the University of Cape Town, where the writers' circle meets regularly, is currently ranked foremost among African universities, making it what the promotional discourse of the institution has called 'world-class in Africa'. What is it like to be a knowledge-maker in this place? Where to start with the layers of inequality, precarity and persistent hope? This university is starkly privileged in the periphery, a university that clings to the mountainside, a nest of neoclassical buildings behind what was once a statue of imperialist Cecil John Rhodes. Before it was taken down in 2015 in the #RhodesMustFall student-led protests, the statue faced North, on a plinth bearing an inscription from Rudyard Kipling's poem for Cape Town that reads 'I dream my dream, by rock and heath and pine, Of Empire to the northward'. A roughly constructed plywood box painted grey now covers the plinth. The protest movements, #RhodesMustFall, which foregrounded the alienation of historically excluded first generation black students from the curriculum, and #FeesMustFall, against economic exclusion, recalibrated the higher education landscape, re-allocating funding and inserting a new discourse of decolonisation that has challenged the widespread use of a narrow version of transformation stripped down to numbers of black bodies in higher education. The removal of the statue has stimulated a literature that I only touch on in this Introduction.[3]

The protests reached beyond the still-recent post-apartheid struggle, resonating with a longer struggle that includes slavery and colonialism and their consequences. These after-effects are felt in a pervasive coloniality – the sociocultural formations left behind after formal colonisation is over (Maldonado-Torres, 2007). The University, like other historically white, English-speaking, liberal universities in South Africa, hid behind its status in what Joan Tronto calls 'privileged irresponsibility'[4] with a blindness to the inequalities in our position as high status in the global south. Something was profoundly wrong with the way that post-apartheid 'transformation' was working itself out as South African higher education morphed from the divided and divisive system under apartheid into the market-oriented university. Historically excluded black students entered the system in significantly larger numbers, but without shifting the inequalities related to class, language and curriculum (Cooper, 2015). Salim Badat (2009) and Jonathan Jansen (2009) are among those to see the complexity of the crisis building before the #MustFall protests revealed some of the tensions in the system. In the wake of the protests, Achille Mbembe (2016: 32–33) points to this crisis and its impact on the knowing subject:

> We all seem to agree that there is something anachronistic, something entirely is wrong with a number of institutions of higher learning in South Africa [...] . Western epistemic traditions are traditions that claim detachment of the known from the knower. They rest on a division between mind and world, or between reason and nature as an ontological a priori. They are traditions in which the knowing subject is enclosed in itself and peeks out at a world of objects and produces supposedly objective knowledge of those objects. The knowing subject is thus able to know the world without being part of that world and he or she is by all accounts able to produce knowledge that is supposed to be universal and independent of context. The problem – because there is a problem indeed – with this tradition is that it has become hegemonic.

Clearly the formal archive has the power to silence and to hurt, as many of the stories from the circle will illustrate. The sense of alienation that comes with writing seen as decontextualised skill, which asks postgraduate scholars to produce knowledge in a way that knows the world without being part of it, has consequences: frameworks, modes of inquiry and writing conventions imported from settings shaped by colonial power, in English, are important as they enable a global conversation, but at what cost? And what would it take to disrupt this? It's complicated. Mbembe for one is worried about how alternatives may produce new hegemonies such as how narrow versions of a 'retrogressive' Africanisation might shrink and earth the knowledge project in new ways, rather than deepen and widen it (2016: 34). In his critique of epistemic coloniality that ensues from this notion of universalism from a single (European/northern/western) viewpoint, Mbembe explores epistemic diversity through the idea of the 'pluriversity' offered by a range of decolonial South American scholars. He advocates an embrace of knowledge-making *via a horizontal strategy of openness to dialogue among different epistemic traditions* (2016: 37, original emphasis). This imagining of knowledge-making through a horizontal strategy of openness resonates with the refigured interaction I envisage between the trace and formal archives as expressed in the idea of surface tension, with elements stretched out alongside one another on a plane.

The critique of epistemic coloniality expressed in postcolonial and decolonial scholarship is an important current in this book on writing from a postgraduate circle. These ideas are brought in by the postgraduate scholars who come to the circle, and they also inform the theoretical ideas and concepts that I explore in bringing different epistemic traditions to this inquiry. The difference between the post- and decolonial approaches is hard to define: Sabelo Ndlovu-Gatsheni (2015: 491) usefully argues that they 'converge and diverge across genealogies, trajectories and horizons'. He writes of a family of approaches making up decolonial work which is more disruptive in spirit than postcoloniality which he sees as more cosmopolitan (2015: 491). The difference between post- and decoloniality is best summed up for me by the prefixes, post- and de-. I first encountered Steve Biko's work on Black Consciousness after the Soweto Uprisings of 1976; postcolonial work in literature and cultural studies, like Edward Said (1979) and Homi Bhabha (1994), is now mainstream having emerged from European structuralist critique that straddles contradiction and recognises that while alienation is never far away, there are always pathways, but there is always an ontological risk. Decoloniality re-emerged strongly in South Africa after the #MustFall protests to signal a directly activist engagement that disrupts deeply embedded coloniality in institutions. The Southern reflectory that I give shape to in this book is informed by these currents as well as others to enable both critique of epistemic coloniality and also to bring forth resources to imagine alternatives.

Writing as Inquiry

More recently in my thinking about language and literacy, affect theory and the work of Deleuze and Guattari (1987) have offered resources for the exploration of writing and knowledge-making. They centre on the idea of emergence, not as a trajectory towards a norm, but as always-already about life where it is lived – in the body and in the thickness of the present. Rather than following the structures of power as sedimented in official archives and convention, I am first of all interested in the conditions for possibility and how the circle alerts me to these conditions where writing is concerned. Gail Boldt and Kevin Leander (2020: 2) look to affect theory to get away from what have become static notions of literacy to find new ways of conceptualising 'who counts as literate and what counts as literacy'. Affect is the property of bodies acting upon one another – body here understood as 'not limited to humans, but includes material objects, spaces, ideas, senses, fantasises, histories and culture' (2020: 3). Following Deleuze and Guattari, these different elements are imagined as spread out on the horizontal plane 'jumbled together from what we imagine to be different categories of life and matter' (2020: 3). So any of the different pieces that are at play in the writers' circle – the words, written or spoken, coffee cups, theories, bodies and their bodily habitus, the accents, policies, fears and laughter – have the potential to affect the possibilities for coming together or for dissolving or imploding, in predictable and unpredictable ways. It's not that critique, power structures and discourses go away, because different combinations of elements may play out to either further centralise or to disperse and open up for innovation. The tension between Mikhail Bakhtin's (1986) concepts of centripetal and centrifugal forces is useful here. A centripetal force is exerted in the way that institutions reduce differences through the creation of norms for meaning. These norms organise and rank through gate-keeping practices that quickly close down differences which then harden as inequalities (Blommaert, 2005). Lillis (2017) uses this argument to engage the idea of the writing imaginary and its shadow in publishing and professional writing. We need to pay attention to these tilting points where it is possible to imagine discursive alternatives (Thesen, 2013).

My interest in emergence, affect and the methods that might enable us to understand and honour these concepts touches on approaches to how writing figures in the process of inquiry to 'develop methods that enable the happening of the social world' (Lury & Wakeford, 2012: 2). The way I see writing as method is more fully explored in Chapter 2, 'The Yellow Folders Draw Me In: Looking for the Trace'.

For now I single out Rosi Braidotti's (2014) idea of writing as a creative and courageous practice of nomadic inquiry for working across and against the clogged critical stasis of the historical moment. Writing is more than a channel of communication or a way to represent reality.

It is a site where subjectivity is constituted.[5] 'Writing is living intensively and inhabiting language as a site of multiple others [...] not just (or even) an instrument of communication, but rather an ontological site of constitution of our shared humanity' (2014: 164). Furthering the idea of an ethics of shared humanity, writing becomes a 'visualization of ethical relationality through the in-depth critique of power' as well as an affirmation of potential (2014: 165). An element in Braidotti's nomadic writer subjectivity is her densely multilingual history in which self-writing is explored in the many crossings she has made between tongues and texts. Braidotti describes her contribution 'as a European nomadic subject moving across variegated landscapes of whiteness, to a debate which black, antiracists, postcolonial and other critical thinkers have put on the map' (2014: 181). The specifics of self-writing have to be named. With a lifetime of diary-writing behind her, it is possible to constitute subjectivity in ways that further empower. In committing to a relational ethics, we can explore subjectivity through writing as a 'visceral gesture' (2014: 163) that places us constantly on the smudged line where self meets other. For me 'variegated landscapes of whiteness' are painfully relevant as, however much I have chafed against my inherited position in this world as a knowledge-maker, my settler colonial antecedents going back four generations are a fact. I am not always convinced that self-writing can be a practice for hopeful subjectivity. This emerging field is inspiring on writing as a mode of inquiry. But it is less rigorous and perhaps more blinkered on seeing academic writing in a global context from the perspective of writers excluded through a process of violent and sustained dispossession.[6]

There will be moments in this book when the different approaches I use clash and seem incoherent though they are linked in a cluster of approaches beginning with the prefix 'post' – postcolonial and post-qualitative within a broadly poststructuralist view of language. I also patch together ideas more widely, from literature, anthropology, the life sciences. But this instability is also a source of meaning-making. Much of why I am so interested in the circle is *because of* the seeming-incommensurability of the brought-along. How do we make sense across disciplines, languages, methodologies, histories, archives as we engage in the circle? Incoherence is invited into the centre of the circle, and this book. So these ideas shape my writing process in this inquiry, but they are also powerful for thinking about the pedagogy of the circle. This is foregrounded in the last two chapters – Chapter 7, '"I remember a few rogue popcorns": Teaching for the Trace', and the Conclusion, 'Knowledge-Making at the Water Point'.

Towards the end of the extended process of authoring this book, Cecile Badenhorst, Brittany Amell and James Burford published their edited book, *Re-imagining Doctoral Writing* (2021). They note that much of the focus on doctoral writing has been on:

… rhetoric, craft, and technique, but essentially ha[s] been steeped in a matter of know-how. In this book, we aim to open a different space to think about doctoral writing. Perhaps we can create space to renew thinking, looking for not only choices that are made but also those that are not made. Can we see the traces, tracks, footprints of what might have been and what could be? (2021: 13)

They call for approaches that open out to embrace a way of thinking about writing that tries to 'see the traces, tracks and footprints of what might have been and what could be'. This book hopes to make a contribution to this conversation about re-imagining doctoral writing by staying with both the trace and the formal archive, commencing from this writers' circle – a place where the trace lives. The trace touches the formal archive right here. At the time of writing, the Thursday Circle is in its 17th year. It has seen many students, three facilitators, different venues, several vice-Chancellors. It has survived (possibly even thrived?) through #MustFall protests and closures and Covid 19 lockdowns. The circle is a clearly designated yet dynamic space that is the crucible for the knowledge-making work in this book, but the trace does not lend itself to being confined: the flow of bodies, texts and ideas spills over beyond the circle.

A Note to the Reader

In this section, I ask the reader to work with me on this journey. Widening and deepening the archive presents challenges for both writers and readers. Joan Turner (2018: 231) asks for a 'a more flexible approach to the uptake of writtenness, breaking the alliance [between writer and reader] with its textual ideologies, notably the expectation of a smooth read'. This may not be a comfortable read as I share this reflection.

The approach I take to writing is immersive in an effort to share the feeling of being there, in the circle and on its edges, rather than looking at it from the outside. The forms of material interspersed across this book include found elements like fragments left over from our gatherings, loosely bundled into folders through the years; rough reflections – spontaneous thoughts jotted in the series of research notebooks I kept while I was facilitator of the circle from 2009 to 2018, written when I felt the need to grasp a moment or a feeling after the circle; memories brought to mind in the process of writing; various drawings, created for different reason. Theoretical resources are woven in across the chapters, but rather than fronting the analysis in each chapter, theory is plaited in as integral to the process of inquiry itself. It is one of the elements in the mix on the plane of affect. I try to interact with theory in a more organic way, getting closer to how we encounter it while thinking and writing over time. In the writing of this book, new lines of inquiry emerged where it was not enough to draw from found 'data' such as the fragments mentioned above. Fresh research inquiries were designed with workshops, interviews and inventive ways of thinking together. These are more recognisable as question-driven research as the views and experiences of others are sought and interpreted. In a spirit of creative inquiry, I try to keep the analysis open as long as possible.

While the Thursday Circle is at the centre of this inquiry, and it continues to be tightly framed as a weekly event with a set day and time, the boundaries are porous in that postgraduates and writing facilitators move in and out of it. The circle is only one of the teaching and learning spaces that my colleagues initiated, eventually ending up with a suite of events, courses and resources guided by a similar philosophy, where ideas were debated and shared. At times, as in Chapter 5 'One Word at a Time: Finding Rhythm in Writing', I step outside of the circle to think with interactions in other courses and workshops that together create a connected web of sense-making action.

A name for the approach I am using here doesn't readily come to mind. It is something like an ethnographic immersion in an extended experience of being part of a writers' circle that seemed to connect with the world in unpredictable but productive ways. It takes up Lillis' (2008: 382) suggestion to explore 'relational rather than denotational or referential' ways to work at the seams between text and context and in so doing to foreground the ontological dimensions in ethnographic research on writing. Anthropologists such as Clifford Geertz and Michael Taussig have explored the problem of representation and the Other in ethnographic work. Over time, I have been influenced by post-qualitative research, backgrounding formal methodology and trying out concepts in order to re-orient thinking (Jackson & Mazzei, 2013; MacLure, 2013; St Pierre, 2019, 2021). I was not familiar with the term post-qualitative at the beginning. My qualitative leanings still come through and my desire to describe and represent life in the circle is important. It is also a concern that while embracing a series of posts-, post-qualitative inquiry seldom includes the post- or de-colonial perspective. I have had to ask new questions about what data means, the power of what is excluded, how to craft a text, whether straightening the line to tell a good story is a betrayal, or an ethical obligation not to leave your reader in the lurch.

Extended ontological inquiries are challenging. I struggled (still struggle) to find the balance between subjective and objective. There are also difficulties with time shifts that have thrown up many obstacles. Insights emerge in the present about past events. The circle is still very much alive although I am no longer a facilitator, and people I met through the circle come back into my life; others that I met in one of the more formal courses I taught alongside, re-appear in the circle even as I write. I still receive weekly emails announcing activities for the next week. The Covid 19 pandemic interrupted and rearranged the circle and the world towards the end of the writing this book, demanding attention. Events and encounters such as these in the present set off new lines of inquiry that overlay previous events. The theoretical resources I draw on here ask questions about how time is configured in the measured university and how it packages not just writing but one's sense of continuity and worth in the knowledge-making process. I try to make it easier for the reader by indicating the different kinds of textual traces that are drawn on here as either reflections from the rough notes that I kept sporadically, or stories and anecdotes that I have reconstructed from memory. In the later chapters, particularly Chapter 4 on laughter and Chapters 6 and 7 which involve looking back at the circle retrospectively, through the eyes of others, I create fresh material through interviews and focus groups.

There are many writers who are exploring the limits of academic writing and its conventions by pushing the discursive boundaries of the formal archive through mixing and alternating languages, genres, and registers. This is discussed in Chapter 3, 'Surface Tension: Writing in the Shadow of the God View'. As innovators at the writing–knowledge-making interface, many of us may be used to reading differently. Those of us who are teachers of academic writing, tasked with supporting research students who are starting out, making their way from imitative pedagogies to knowledge-making frames where one must offer an 'original contribution to knowledge', will have taught courses and modules on academic reading and writing. I have certainly made use of resources and heuristics such as the rhetorical moves for writing abstracts based on John Swales and Christine Feak (2009). I still find them so valuable. This book no doubt leans into the conventions more often than it bends and interrogates them. But where there seems to be confusion – a sudden time shift or data mode or less interpretation than one is used to, a strange structure that does not proceed as expected through the rituals of question, theory, method, analysis, interpretation, a swerve or a dive – I hope readers will find the confusion productive, inviting a fresh, or perhaps unsettling, response.

Ethics: An I is always a We, and a They

The first person in research writing is a trickster. It slides about, torn between fact and fiction, verification, testimony and confession. I have to use it though, to take responsibility for my presence in the circle and for how I interpret it. And in the approach I am using where writing becomes a 'visualization of ethical relationality' (Braidotti, 2014: 165) in both critique and affirmation as a form of inquiry, the pronouns 'we' and 'they' are crucial and present, even in their absence. Pronouns are relational. The writing I is set in motion by a complex meshing with the other in a desire to communicate. But in making my way across the 'landscapes of whiteness' that Braidotti describes, while trying to de-link and distance myself, there are many stumbles, when the I becomes we – people who teach writing/are feeling our way beyond the New Literacy Studies/in the global south/older white woman – and a we anticipates a they, and possibly an Other. It is more-than-human though: the materiality of folders, popcorn on the floor, the haunting of historical voices, the gut feel – are all part of the becoming and of my writing, of the writers' circle and of what we can say about writing and knowledge-making.

Most acutely, there is my responsibility to my colleagues and to students who came to the circle. Although there is one author of this book, there are many voices that are in this text. Three of us have facilitated the Thursday circle over the years. Clement initiated and animated the early circles, with me alongside. At that time, he was doing a PhD on Marxist stylistics in Applied Linguistics/Cultural Studies while employed as a tutor at the Writing Centre. I was a lecturer in Academic Literacies in the Centre for Higher Education Development (where the Writing Centre is located) and was also doing my PhD. It was a difficult time for me professionally. I had been given a chance to initiate a postgraduate writing intervention with tutors in our Writing Centre. I think it was also a difficult time for Clement. After Clement left to join his family in New Zealand, I carried on with the weekly circles. Aditi also worked in the Writing Centre, while doing her PhD in Academic Literacies. I was her supervisor. After joining the circle as a student, she gradually became more involved as a facilitator, taking over my role after I retired. During the pandemic, she successfully moved the circle online, returning to a hybrid practice alternating between online and in person meetings after the pandemic. Aditi and Clement were centrally involved in Chapter 7 where they figure as co-authors.

Some circle members are in the foreground, particularly those who took part in the research inquiries designed in the later chapters. Aditi, Vuyo, Kay, Jo, Elena, Natasha, Tia and Elizabeth in Chapter 4 on laughter; Kay, Siwela and Tia in Chapter 6 about the reflections of three ex-circlers, and in Chapter 7 in which the three facilitators recall moments in the circle. Ellen is a colleague who worked with Clement and me in the early days of the circle. In Chapter 5, I write about Thusi, when I became aware of her presence in the circle during the pandemic. I had previously met Thusi while teaching on a writing course for postgraduates. The names of my colleagues are unchanged, while the names of all the postgraduate scholars who I write about have been changed. Although most opted not to change their names, an uneven naming practice seemed distracting for the reader. It also felt too viscerally personal at times.

The ethical issues are crucial as many students experienced the circle as a safe space. As a group of committed circlers used to say, 'What happens in Vegas stays in Vegas'. As my interest in the life of the circle developed into a formal inquiry with this book in mind, I applied for ethics permission from my faculty ethics committee. Participants knew I was researching the circle as I sometimes brought my writing to the circle for discussion: I brought an extract from the ethics proposal I was to submit to my faculty for the group to comment on. Circlers gave me guidance for drawing up the information and consent form required. In a group email, I wrote to all students who had attended fairly regularly over the years, describing the project and explaining the steps I would take for ethical conduct. I said that if I were to write about students in the rough reflections that I sometimes reconstruct after the circle, or refer substantially to students' projects or written work, I would change their names and identifiers, if they wished, and only proceed with their permission. In the inquiries for the later chapters, I communicated with each group of students separately for each chapter and together we created ethical guidelines for each process of inquiry.[7] All participants read at least one draft of the chapter that concerned them, suggesting changes. Right up to the end of this process of writing, I grappled with 'reflexivities of discomfort' (Pillow, 2003) in deciding how someone is represented or how much subjectivity is necessary or relevant.

The Circle as a Portal to Knowledge-Making: The Chapters

The sequence of chapters in this book suggests a movement outwards from the circle. This echoes the way that while the circle is at the heart of this book, it is also a portal to move beyond it, a threshold space that is always taking us elsewhere. In Chapter 1, I describe and locate the circle, and reflect on what kind of space it is; Chapter 2 explores the methods used in this search for the trace, including how writing is a form of inquiry; Chapter 3 introduces the idea of surface tension to explore the interface between the trace and the god view associated with the formal archive; Chapter 4 steps away from writing in the circle to consider the relationship between laughter and writing; Chapter 5 starts with the circle but goes beyond to explore time and rhythm in writing; the next two chapters look back at the circle retrospectively through interviews with three ex-circlers (Chapter 6) and through the memories of the Aditi, Clement and myself as facilitators (Chapter 7). The final chapter considers the relationship between writing and knowledge-making through the notion of writing as a watery smudge at the interface.

Notes

(1) See Bourdieu *et al.* (1994), Gee (1990), and Ballard and Clanchy (1988). This argument that writing and privilege are intertwined is a core insight in the New Literacy Studies and Academic Literacies traditions discussed in this chapter.

(2) See Lillis *et al.* (2015) for context to Academic Literacies. There is a rich literature in the spirit of Academic Literacies in South Africa. The strands of critical scholarship on language and literacy in learning, particularly in resistance to apartheid, flow into the movement as described in Lillis *et al.* It is not easy to delineate a 'tradition' in South Africa, partly because the term Academic Literacy(ies) is often used in an uncritical way, to describe access courses in which historically excluded students are

assimilated into mainstream. There is a significant body of work that challenges how the deficit discourse is constituted at the intersection of language, class and race in higher education. See for example Bangeni and Kapp (2017), and Boughey and McKenna (2016). Cecilia Jacobs has done powerful research on disciplinary collaboration. See her paper on outsiders looking in (2005). It is also difficult to generalise as institutions have taken up the concept in a variety of ways that reflect their histories. In our edited book (Thesen & Van Pletzen, 2006), we describe the emergence of Academic Literacies at the University of Cape Town as a response to wider contextual issues. Lynn Coleman (2018) works with lecturers in the University of Technology context to challenge deficit conceptions of students.

(3) Mbembe's (2016) article cited here is in a special issue of the journal *Arts and Humanities in Higher Education*. The special issue, 'State of urgency: The Humanities in South Africa' was put together to explore events a year after #RMF and #FMF. Francis Nyamnjoh's book, *#RhodesMustFall: Nibbling at Resistant Colonialism in South Africa* was also published in 2016. Later research broadens analysis: Kelly Gillespie and Leigh-Anne Naidoo (2019) look at #RMF in the context of student protest since the Soweto Uprising of 1976 while Buhle Khanyile (2021) explores the meanings of violence raised by the protests, and Wahbie Long (2021) critiques the movement psychoanalytically as his book puts South Africa 'on the couch'. More widely, there is a rich collection of texts engaging with issues of decoloniality in Applied Linguistics, Carolyn McKinney and Pam Christie's edited book (2022) focuses on language, literacy and decoloniality mainly from South Africa, centring on the University of Cape Town. Sinfree Makoni for example describes the sociolinguistic intellectual currents he is part of in different ways, under umbrella terms such as Southern Multilingualisms (2020, with Alistair Pennycook), Southern Epistemologies, Southernising Sociolinguistics (2022, Bassey Antia and Sinfree Makoni), Black Linguistics (2003, Ball *et al.* (eds)) thus asking questions from within different conversations that are all broadly decolonial in intent.

(4) See also Zembylas *et al.* (2014) for Tronto's notion of privileged irresponsibility (see for example Tronto, 1993) to reconceptualise the ethics of care, with strong reference to South African higher education.

(5) This insight about writing as a site for the constitution of subjectivities was powerfully though differently made in New Literacy Studies/Academic Literacies work through Roz Ivanic's research (Clark & Ivanic, 1997; Ivanic, 1998; Ivanic & Camps 2001) where it was used to argue against deficit readings of student writing.

(6) Examples of this struggle for self-writing in an alien form are Rozena Maart's 'Exordium: Writing and the relation: From textual coloniality to South African Black Consciousness' (2014) in which Maart wrestles with English to make the colonising tongue a site for the constitution of subjectivity. She draws inspiration from Steve Biko's seminal text *I write what I like* (1978). Mbembe's *On the Postcolony* (2001) is a brilliant account of the challenges of African self-writing in the Francophone postcolony. His creative process is described in 'Achille Mbembe in conversation with Isabel Hofmeyr' (Hofmeyr, 2006).

(7) For example, at the workshop on laughter described in Chapter 4, I handed out the general ethics participation and consent form that I had previously circulated in an email to a selected group of committed circlers. As anticipated, only a handful of circlers had contacted me to give their general consent. The workshop gave me a second opportunity to reach participants. Those who had not yet signed, did so in the workshop. I quote from the general form:

> Consent: The ethical challenges are substantial. We have always tried to make the circle a safe space and a research project can disrupt that. In bringing the circle to life, I may refer to some aspect of your research, such as a draft brought to the circle, or reconstruct a discussion in the circle. I will take the following steps to respect the circle space:

- I will use pseudonyms and try to anonymise research projects using protocols for 'de-identification'
- If I refer to your contribution or to your work beyond an anonymised passing mention, I will only do so with your permission
- For taking part in workshops later this year, I will write to you separately and negotiate ethical boundaries and consent for each activity
- If needed, I will ask for guidance on how I have written about the circle from circle members as well as members of my faculty ethics committee
- You can withdraw at any stage of the process

The form ends, 'If you have any comments or concerns, I'd love to hear from you. Ethical research is a process – there are bound to be aspects that I have not thought of, which we can discuss further'.

For the workshop on laughter, I told participants that I was not recording the workshop, that I would reconstruct notes after the workshop and share the draft chapter with participants. All circlers gave me their sheets of graph paper and freewrites, with permission to use them. I suggested drafting a new consent form, but the group did not think this was necessary.

For the individual interviews in Chapter 6, each interview included a discussion about ethics. Kay, Siwela and Tia each read drafts of the chapter and responded with comments that I incorporated. Some of these are discussed in Chapter 6.

1 A Threshold Space of Difference: Introducing the Thursday Circle

Rats are rhizomes. Burrows are too, in all their functions of shelter, supply, movement, evasion, and breakout.

Deleuze and Guattari (1987: 7) *A Thousand Plateaus*

This chapter sketches the Thursday writers' circle and its practices through a series of images and reconstructions from reflections jotted down in the series of notebooks that I kept through the years when I was facilitator. I describe the main practices that sustained the circle and engage with the problematics of the notion of safe space, suggesting instead that ideas such as brave space or the Deleuzian idea of nomadic space are more productive for this inquiry. I end the chapter by thinking of the circle as a water point as postgraduate writers are always between, or in the middle, never really arriving, always becoming.

Safe Space?

What kind of space is the Thursday writers' circle? What practices thrive here? In our efforts as facilitators to feel our way into what we were doing in the early days of the circle, we thought of it as a safe space[1] in contrast to the dominant image of research writing as lonely, technical and alienating. Over time, the concept of safe space has not always made sense to me as a facilitator of the circle, because although we always tried to create an accepting environment where participants don't leave themselves at the door, it seldom felt secure or predictable. With coursework teaching, academics work with a cohort and a rhythm of attendance, knowledge coverage and assessment. The circle is instead unpredictable, flickering, itinerant, sometimes dragging. Facilitators are not sure how many people will be there on the day, who will stay, what they will take away from the circle. There is no assessment to check on progress. Aditi, Clement and I shared and alternated roles as both facilitators and participants, sometimes bringing our own work-in-progress for critique. The feeling of vulnerability never went away.

However, for all its felt limitations, the ideal of a safe space was a powerful imaginary in the early days of the circle. My sketch in Figure 1.1 gives a glimpse of the circle as a utopian space.

It is a drawing I made for a poster[2] when we first advertised writers' circles in 2006. It expresses the idea of an ideal writing space: social, embodied, gently held with the expert's role unmarked. The items in the assemblage of small things – cups, pens, paper, eats – are all there. The written texts are secondary to the co-presence and sense of involvement conveyed in the body language. It is tight enough to hold, but loose enough to let the air in.

Our choice to use the word circle to describe what we do, rather than for example group, evokes a spatial, bounded concept. It also suggests a sense of belonging and possibly of containment, of holding what happens beyond the circle at bay. A glance at the chapter titles in Aitchison and Guerin's *Writing Groups for Doctoral Education and Beyond* (2014) reflects these spatial metaphors in terms of physical, communicative and emotional space. Positive, possibly gendered descriptors such as 'embrace', 'gift', 'intimate' suggest an emotional content, while physical space is referenced in the words 'circle', 'retreat', 'studio' 'cafes' and 'crowds', all a counterpoint to the loneliness of drawn-out isolated processes as well as to other potentially sterile classroom spaces.

What might it feel like for people who have been part of the circle, or have stood on the edge of it before changing their minds and deciding that it wasn't for them, or re-joining after a break? Perhaps a feeling of exposure and imminent threat is inherent in the idea of safe space. A sense of vulnerability if not danger was clearly there for Max, a student who at the supervisor's suggestion, sought help with their writing. Recalling our meeting all these years later, the circle, of all the writing-related fora available, seemed like a good possibility for finding confidence after an extended period of being unable to write. When we met to discuss writing support options, I

Figure 1.1 An early drawing of the writers' circle as an ideal safe space

made what I thought was a helpful connection to a regular participant in the circle. Max went quiet when asked if he knew the student. Slowly I came to understand more of the backstory. Max was in a witness protection programme: at this stage his identity as a postgraduate student was more of an alibi to keep him safe than a chance to contribute to knowledge-making in the sense anticipated by the academy. The circle would not be a safe space. Just when I think I get it, when I can offer professional expertise and the response that will do the least harm, the screen shifts as if to ambush the limits and limitations of my understanding, both then, in listening to him at the time, and years later in remembering the detail of events. In Moeain Arend's (2014) study of adult learners returning to university to enrol for research degrees, he highlights that for many postgraduates, 'it was hardly about writing', in the words of Sahdia, the postgraduate scholar he interviews. There is often a deep personal quest behind the desire to do a research degree. For Sahdia, it was the desire post-apartheid to give voice to community in 'a domain that had suppressed and darkened its rich colour before' (2013: 227). For Max, having been a competent and brave professional, it might be about whispering, hiding, history, camouflage, and ultimately shelter as he moved on to complete a master's degree with the support of a writing mentor – a volunteer who worked with postgraduate researchers for no pay. Research writing, and what looks like writer's block, are tangled up in complex and evolving journeys.

The exploration in this chapter of what the circle felt like for me as facilitator and how I imagined it for others is drawn from reflections over an extended period. These reflections were written erratically, part of my positionality as facilitator trying to make a go of this new practice with all its uncertainties. They tend to express questions and doubts rather than certainties. They were started before I had formally committed to a research project about the circle. The chapter also draws from memories of interactions with students like Max, exploratory writing with theoretical concepts woven in, as well as attempts to step outside of the circle to defamiliarise my sense of the space, to think of what it *might be* as I venture further from the idea of safe space. It is written in a spirit of 'ethical relationality' that I think is what Braidotti (2014) has in mind in her idea of nomadic inquiry.

Event

Below is a reconstruction of a circle event that evolved from reflections after trying to make sense of a circle that had been shot through with tensions and possibilities.

Today Jo has offered to bring something from her data. We are a cosy group by this stage, mainly women. I have been conscious that we are perhaps a little too cosy. Patrice is no longer coming. Why? Should I send him an email to ask if he's OK? There are PhD and master's students at different stages, in different disciplines. Elizabeth is close to finishing her study of carers of terminally ill cancer patients. She and Jo are disciplinary worlds apart but are both using versions of phenomenology. They share readings, talk about Heidegger; we joke about 'authenticity'. We share the ups and downs of Jo's PhD on preparing nurses in intensive care units to talk about their experiences related to the deaths of patients under their care. The link between her life and her research topic is sharp at this point. She is returning to the circle after the recent death of her mother and has brought a cake to share with us.

She walks into the room shyly, cake in hand, holds back as she sees two new circle members in the room. Fehmi is a historian. Last week we read a translation of an article he is writing on typology and knowledge paradigms. I have been struggling with how to offer constructive critique and am worried that I misunderstand him and might be steering talk away from what he really wants to say. Langa is also new in the group. He is close to finishing his PhD on land and democracy in the rural Eastern Cape. He is an activist and ex-teacher with a commitment to participatory knowledge-making processes. I know he sees history very differently from Fehmi. I have a moment of anxiety: how will I knit this changing group together yet again? I ask Adam to describe what we do: 'Everyone gives and everyone gets' he says. 'There's no "homework"; just bring two pages'. We go around the circle, introducing ourselves quickly and putting a name to our projects.

Jo clears her throat. She tells us that she has not yet met with her supervisor. He is keen to make contact but she isn't ready to bring her work to him. She shows us her students' drawings representing death and dying in the ICU wards. One is particularly challenging. It shows a child lying on a bed, wrapped in bandages. The carer, a young male nurse, has drawn a self-portrait of himself standing next to the bed, forming a striking vertical line as he seems to look at us, with large tears rolling down his cheeks. Jo explains how the drawing fits in to her data and then reads an interview with the student nurse in which he describes the drawing. The bandages cover burn wounds from a fire in the child's home and the boy's mother seems to have been responsible. He talks about the bond that developed between him and the boy. Jo reads for about 10 minutes. We hear her interview questions and the student nurse's responses. She stumbles as she reads some of his words. 'The responses are a bit incoherent', she tells us, 'English isn't his first language'. There is silence in the circle. Then the questions begin. What had the boy's mother done? I try to steer the conversation away from a judgement of the mother. There is relief as Langa asks about the interviews. We are now shifting into the stuff of research. He asks how the formality of the set-up with the young student nurse, and his awareness of Jo as his lecturer, affected what he said? What about language differences? The nurse has had to express complex emotions in English which is not his primary language. We talk about how incoherent we, as researchers, sound in interviews. We wonder whether we can treat spoken language in the same way as written language. We talk about the status of the drawings in a constructive critique that expresses our rigour and ethical awareness.

Towards the end of our two hours together, Elizabeth mimics our different responses to Jo's introduction of her data. She goes around the room, faces us one by one, acting out disbelief, sorrow, relief, scepticism and scholarly concern in turn. Laughter unites us. A few weeks later, Jo tells us that she has written a draft analysis and shown it to her supervisor. He likes it.

This sketch shares the discomfort – for me as facilitator and also as I imagine the discomforts for the participants – and also the joys of the circle. The sketch highlights the circle as a space of difference, not in the sense that all experiences are seen as equal and we are in this together, but in a much more risky and even dangerous sense. What happens in the circle is unpredictable. The way people are called to open themselves, give and withhold judgement as they carry their histories, is much more reminiscent of what Brian Arao and Kristi Clemens (2013) call a brave rather than a safe space. A brave space needs some way of holding difference so that it does not overwhelm either writers or facilitators. It reframes social justice pedagogy 'to emphasize the need for courage rather than the illusion of safety' (2013: 141).

We have called the circle a rehearsal space (Chihota & Thesen, 2014). In a talk we gave on the emerging pedagogy of the circle, a colleague questioned this term, referring to their experience of ballet rehearsals which often worked back from a clear, well-established notion of the product. The rehearsal metaphor is not really a space for risk-taking, they said. It implies something uni-directional, a channelling towards an ideal that if not pre-determined, is strongly shaped by the director. But what if there is no script or the script has yet to be created, or if the whole performance is seen as a collaborative process from the outset? There is no single author, no lone supervisor, but a collective. In the circle, the postgraduates are doing their own steering, choosing what, if anything, to bring to the circle; choosing what to say, whether to come. Some postgraduate scholars are also academics. For the facilitator, absence is not an option. It is essential to pitch up, to carry institutional memory, to create a shell that may be inhabited by some forms of writing life. A necessary script-of-sorts evolved for holding the slippage between the familiar and the unfamiliar. It is in this slippage that creativity lies.

Practices in the Writers' Circle

The reconstruction of the event above is an expression of the weave and texture of a particular meeting that had stood out for me. Here I focus on four elements of practice that evolved in the circle over time: the weekly email announcement, participant information form, the practice of bringing two pages that are at the heart of circle practices, and the warm-up activities that facilitators, and sometimes students, introduced in most but not all sessions.

For the most part, the circle works like this. Everyone is welcome. There is no formally constituted cohort, and little visible hierarchy. There are Honours students in their fourth year, master's, PhDs who may also be academics. Some scholars stay on as they transition to finding work beyond the PhD. Some pop in to see what it's about. Occasionally postgraduates join while registered at other universities. Disciplinary differences are a given and a point of entry into a conversation where you are the expert on your research.

In spite (or because) of the openness of attendance, the circle is tightly structured in time-space. Participants know that we meet once a week throughout the year, pausing for short breaks in July (the winter vacation) and for six weeks over the summer break. We meet at 3pm on a Thursday afternoon. The room described in the reconstruction above has a central wooden table, tea and coffee laid out on a tea trolley, high windows, an aluminium sink that suddenly gurgles for no reason. Without too much planning there is always food on the table: popcorn, grapes, biscuits, cake. Also seemingly unplanned is the porous nature of attendance. Postgraduates hear by word of mouth, or when the circle is mentioned at scheduled workshops or short courses for students. Some come for company and support; others, like Max, are advised to come by their supervisors. The deficit discourse mentioned in the Introduction is never far away, so students who attend have often been advised to get help with their writing. At some point a second-generation of circlers began to attend as a recently graduated PhD, now a supervisor, who had been in the circle as a student, recommended that her students attend.

There are some administrative elements that add necessary spine to the radically open pedagogy of the circle. One is the weekly email sent to all names on the Thursday Writers' Circle email list. Briefly, the emails are written by the facilitator. They are sent out before the circle and do two things: summarise what happened at the most recent circle the previous week and announce what is coming up next. The 'what next?' element is usually signalled in the subject line of the email, most often to include the name(s) of the writer whose work we will be looking at on Thursday. So a recent email has 'Carl's lit review – mapped' for a circle where Carl wanted to share a diagram developed to map the structure of his literature review. Another is headed 'Going backstage – Zandile and Tia' when two PhD's wanted space to talk about the backstory to their respective research projects. The agenda for the next circle is usually decided at the end of the circle. Students request sessions in advance, using the circle as a planning space as they work towards more high-stakes audiences.

There is also a form for participant details that is printed out and circulated towards the end of each session. If the facilitator forgets to hand the paper around, someone will usually ask, 'Can I sign before I leave?'. The participant details form seems to be more important to participants than to the facilitators. At the end of the circle, students write down their names, degree, key research concepts, stage they are at, and immediate plans. The forms were introduced in part for bureaucratic reasons, to count the number of attendances (so we could report impact) and to understand the patterns when we first started the Thursday Circle. We look at these only occasionally. For the participants, they seem to serve a different function. By signing, they are saying 'I was there: I was not wasting my time'. This seems to serve a ritual purpose, enabling students to be part of something that has continuity, and to make a contribution by giving feedback to a writer, but also noting the changes (or not) in their own research journeys. Perhaps a hesitation about a shift in a key concept or noticing that they are no longer writing that they are in the 'analysing data' stage provides a sense that something is changing. It is also potentially a form of surveillance in the Foucauldian sense: signing, committing to next steps is a sort of cop-in-the-head activity (Foucault, 1977): students have taken on their own journeys and self-regulate with little external cajoling. Kay, who graduated with a PhD and continued to come to the circle after graduation, admitted that for a year, she had written almost nothing. Then suddenly, the gates opened and she completed her PhD in a comfortable four years. In Chapter 6, Kay shares more about this time in her life.

Two pages and no homework

At the heart of our textual practices is the notional two pages that students bring when it is their turn for getting feedback. The point of the two pages is that no-one has to do any peer reading or 'homework' before a circle: the contribution is *inside* the circle when we all read and respond to a short piece that is contextualised by the writer. No homework is a cornerstone of our practice. It means that all of us come to the circle without anxiety and shame that we might have let people down by failing to read lengthy pieces in advance. This is important for postgraduates who feel uneasy about giving feedback when they are not making progress in their own writing. Reading together recasts reading as a form of communal generosity rather than individual obligation. The nature of the short piece varies. Most often it is a section that a writer is wrestling with – working with literatures, motivating an unusual methodological approach, situating oneself in an introduction in a context that has changed since the research process began, choosing unusual forms of evidence. Individuals innovate. So Kay once brought a whole chapter, giving each person in the circle two pages of the whole to read; Tia and Tumi innovated by bringing two pages of raw data so the reading involved circlers in data coding. Both scholars included this engagement in the methodology write-up of their theses. Interactions were more than social – they were also epistemic. Ellen for example acknowledges the circle for being a 'forum in which to develop ideas' for her PhD thesis. This is explored as a story from the interface in Chapter 3. Others used the space to prepare conference presentations, blog entries, funding applications, presentations for job interviews.

These two-pagers are crucial as they are a portal for doing the edgework (Lyng, 1990) that loosely stitches the practices of the circle to the wider world of knowledge-making. For Lyng, edgework is relational, a way of exploring the fine lines in the dialectic between spontaneity and constraint that are at the heart of agentive action: 'In abstract terms, edgework is best understood as the boundary between order and disorder, form and formlessness' (1990: 839). The two pages work well at the interface between different elements as authors shuttle between private strivings and public outcomes in their processes of becoming. The two pages are a gateway, like tickets that give entry to a threshold space that is always about an in-between, travelling between two places, never arriving, always in the making. Instead of handing your ticket in at the door, you share it with others, and take it away again at the end, but with lots of embellishments, endorsements and queries in the form of spoken and written commentary.

Serious play

An optional element in the circles is what Clement initially called the warm-up, a sharing, focusing activity that often bares some kind of connection to what we are directing our attention to in the circle that week. These may be introduced by one of the participants who shares a way of organising readings, a new bit of software, a heuristic for thinking about page and document design, a post from a blog for postgraduate writers (Thesis Whisperer, The Doctoral Writing SIG or Patter). Quite often these brief warm-ups involve humour or parody, or a serious discussion such as the one we had about the Bad Writing award given to feminist philosopher Judith Butler, plus her defence of her academic writing style. These activities represent a range of stances on academic writing, from normative 'this is the way it is' activities to more parodic, transgressive approaches that invert and ask questions about the very nature of the thing we are all pursuing. These turn seriousness on its head. Humour is a key part of the circle. Normative and disruptive elements are placed side by side and sometimes explicitly juxtaposed.

There are also more subtle values and practices that emerge and recede as the group changes, such as the motif that everybody gives and everybody gets, meaning that even if it's not your turn to have your work valued and scrutinised, you receive something by offering your critique and witnessing other's journeys. Participants have commented on the way their curiosity and general knowledge expanded with exposure to others' research projects. While painful and frustrating experiences with supervisors and ethics permission gatekeepers are shared, scholars do not often complain about supervisors. I sometimes speak from the supervisor's position, sharing the challenges and dilemmas that arise from a system under pressure. As facilitators, we are also caught up in the imperatives of the count culture with its pressure to complete and publish while the clock is ticking loudly. Postgraduate scholars know that facilitators know some of the supervisors personally and are in a position to feed back to the structures that organise the postgraduate space at the University. Sometimes we channel requests from students on difficulties with the formalities of the examination process, such as the clunky policy introduced with the mandatory use of plagiarism detection software on thesis submission. Thus a mixture of the serious and the comical animates the circle, enabling participants to see different subjectivities in action, while staying close to the knowledge-making project. The alchemy of both laughter and what Clement called 'the august' are invited and in play. That postgraduate students in the circle can come when they feel like it, return after an absence, laugh or cry, is what the space is about, and what lends itself to the ludic, desire-driven edge where the trace lives, on the cusp between formal and informal. Knowledge is more than what gets sedimented in the formal archive.

Hold on, This Doesn't Sound Right …

At this point, my description of the writing circle sounds too idealistic. Perhaps it is the detail and the use of the present tense that makes it sound too cosy. Perhaps it sounds utopian because it is a symptom of just how dystopian much of the world of academic research writing is with students' struggles with alienation and voice. And my university is nested in a complex and fraught sociopolitical setting where fault lines of raced, classed, gendered and ableist privilege are reinscribed in every moment. Of course the circle is part of this. Perhaps we who have been tasked to 'help students write' could think of the circle as *hetero*topian in Foucault's sense, rather than utopian. Heterotopias are sanctioned spaces, like cemeteries, ships, circuses, libraries, museums and circuses, that are places of difference, still tethered to the messiness of practices, policies and institutions all around them. Beth Lord (2006) draws on Foucault 1998 to describe heterotopias as:

> [...] absolutely central to a culture but in which the relations between elements of a culture are suspended, neutralized, or reversed. Unlike utopias, heterotopias are real places 'designed into the very institution of society' in which all the other real emplacements of a culture are 'at the same time, represented, contested, and reversed, sorts of places that are outside all places, although they are actually localizable'. (2006: 1)

In an exploration of what kind of space the circle could be, writing teachers could think of spaces such as the circle as allowed to be different, but only up to a point, in relation to other institutional and discursive spaces.

These heterotopic spaces mirror, comment on or refract other, usually more normative spaces. But I need to go further. UCT is a *particular* university. I am acutely aware of the disjuncture between my comfy description of circle practices and how national and institutional histories impact on the life of the circle. In the Introduction, I touched on how the call to decolonise the University disrupted conventions to show up hidden histories. Below I expand on how the University's institutional niche in South African higher education brought the circle into being in ways that both enable and constrain.

Outside/In: The Writers' Circle in Context

While the circle is radically open and seemingly spontaneous, patterns of attendance and who seeks help are socially produced and constrained as inside and outside bleed into each other. This is expressed in the range of concepts such as chronotope (Bakhtin, 1981), timescape (Adam, 2004) and spatiality (especially Kraftl (2016)) all of which tell us that spaces are made discursively in processes that are historical, relational, affective and material. At the broad level, the social structure of the postgraduate cohort at UCT is already historically skewed. Most importantly, particularly in the early life of the circle, the low numbers of black South African students who crack through the glass ceiling to excel as senior undergraduates and eventually become tenured academics who will supervise the next generation of researchers has been a matter of great concern. This ramifies outwards into major questions about the knowledge-making project in Southern African higher education. This raises the question of who the new knowledge-makers will be[3] and what knowledges they will draw on and contribute to, and in what discursive forms.

The institutional history of the circle is also significant. The circle began in 2006 as a response to policy shifts to change the shape and size of the higher education system by merging institutions (Council on Higher Education, 2000). The main impact of the policy was to create three types of universities in an attempt to break away from rigid apartheid classifications along lines of race, class and language. A small number of universities, including UCT, historically privileged by their structural whiteness, were let off the hook and given the opportunity to differentiate by focusing on their research strengths.[4] UCT took on the identity of a research-intensive university, which would increase the number of postgraduates, at the cost of growth in undergraduate numbers. While postgraduate provision had previously been seen as a matter for the academic department and faculty, the shift to embrace a research-intensive identity meant that the production of research and of researchers was centralised administratively. At the same time, an image of UCT as 'distinguished' was emerging within a nascent neoliberal institutional culture that valued research as a commodity in terms that can be counted.

This moment was an opportunity for us to open up spaces for alternative pedagogies for research writing. As Doreen Starke-Meyerring (2014: 65) says, 'Like all practices of doctoral education, doctoral writing, including writing groups, exists in institutional environments, which [...] are stubbornly consistent in one respect; they tend to keep writing marginalised and shrouded in silence'. The cross-faculty structure I worked in, the Centre for Higher Education Development, was asked to assist with what was deemed to be a major problem. In a survey of senior academics and administrators at this time, supporting student writing was identified as a challenge to supervisors, particularly with the admission of international postgraduates who had not come through local undergraduate disciplinary taproots. 'Writing' became a risk-object that had to be managed (Thesen & Cooper, 2014) typically through outsourcing to the literacy people like ourselves, with our often demeaned 'generic' work. Our team started offering writers' circles through our well-established Writing Centre. We felt that at undergraduate level, the one-on-one pedagogy of the writing consultation complemented the large lecture cohort, but at the postgraduate level, what seemed to be missing was a more communal, low stakes writing space. So we opened the door, and waited to see who came.

It was clear from the outset that attendance patterns and the dynamics of the circle are an expression of how space is socially formed. We did not keep track of the demographics of the group in terms of race, gender and nationality (the three main descriptors used in South African higher education equity planning). But it is clear in the reflections below, written to give form to the issues, thoughts and feelings arising for me, that I was troubled by how the group was constituted while I was facilitator. My reflections express doubts and questions – moments of being troubled more than moments of joy and discovery and camaraderie. They help to critique the notion of safe space.

Changing Spaces

Reflection 1[5]

We meet at the Slug and Lettuce for a 'cheeky pint' well into December to mark the end of the year. I am nervous. Will everyone feel comfortable? Who have I excluded? Gita arrives, and then Harry. I haven't seen him for ages. He asks, are there any men in the group? Am I right that when Clement was here, we had far more men? I run through the people I can remember. Is Harry the only white guy to come for any length of time?

Reflection 2

I think back on those meetings in Aditi's flat while we couldn't meet on campus during #rmf. Aditi's flat got too small, so we met at Co-Co [café popular with students and academics]. It was too full. Classes, meetings spilled over into cafés during the protests. We moved next door to the

> *Tea House, which was empty. I remember that Honor arrived late and sat next to me, listened while some spoke about the 'incivility' (that word was doing the rounds) of students during the protests. She spoke quietly about a protest where women showed their breasts. She explains it's about having nothing left to lose. I can see she is hurt. I don't know how to keep the space from collapsing. She doesn't come back. I write to ask if she is OK. 'All good'.*

The concerns raised in my reflections above are precipitated by a change of space – in the first entry, the suggestion of a pub as a venue for an end of year gathering and in the second, the search for an off-campus space during the #MustFall protests of 2015 and 2016. The porousness between the circle and the wider social context was vividly brought to life during the student protests as we sought alternative spaces for the circle, particularly when a controversial interdict prohibited students from being on campus. The question of who comes to which events, who speaks and why, is never far away. The protests put decolonial thought on the institutional agenda, sharpening my awareness of how the circle could be functioning as a safe space for white privilege was masking patterns of the racial ordering of difference. Stepping outside of the familiar physical space of the circle also nudges me to think differently, to estrange myself from routine events.

Most campus venues are more-or-less 'neutral' space (our regular venue had the bland title of the 5th Floor Meeting Room) but choosing off-campus venues, especially when the campus was closed during the protests, was loaded with concerns about access and what constituted hospitable space. These reflections express discomfort in my role as facilitator as I try to negotiate spaces where whiteness intersects with gender and class. In the first note I am defensive about gender, in the second I am uncomfortable with the discussion on 'civility' which had become a trope among many academics as they struggled to make sense of the shock of the protests. I bit my tongue, not knowing how to intervene, but Honor speaks quietly to break the silence. I recall that there were only women at that meeting in Aditi's flat. A feature of the circle through the years is that there are usually more women.[6] There seems to be a gendered dimension to making oneself available for support, construed as 'care'. But gender also intersects with spaces of whiteness and the extent to which they exclude. This was a constant concern while I was facilitator.

Some years after these entries, during the Covid 19 pandemic, another change of space occurred when the circle was altered by online participation. This space-time shift helps to think about the circle in a different time, through Aditi's eyes after she had become facilitator. Aditi had been running the circle successfully since the beginning of the pandemic, working in an environment that was entirely online. Online teaching had controversially been given a boost by the years of the #MustFall protests, as the University began to adopt online learning, making resources available to try to keep the curriculum afloat, leap-frogging the politics of the situation by relocating everything to virtual space. Of course virtual space is always grounded – grounded in a place that does or does not have reliable wifi, have data to pay for time to access, and in a history that gives students an orientation to studying online. Aditi shared her experience[7] of a recent circle that had gone wrong after she was unable to facilitate via a video link because of a power failure due to rolling blackouts on the national electricity grid. The two pages to be shared on the day involved giving feedback on research about the controversial ban on alcohol in South Africa during the pandemic. Unable to host the event, members of the circle impro-vised and gave extensive email feedback that Aditi describes as 'border-ing on harsh' as the email format seemed to make the responders 'tone deaf'. Here the rituals of real-time verbal responses break down with defensive comments that Aditi later has to repair, reminding partici-pants of the ethos of the writers' circle. For a moment, the holding ritu-als seem to have broken down, making the space unsafe.

So in an organic way, the meaning of the circle space was tested as physical space changed. In the next section I try to explore the space by defamiliarising pedagogic space as a creative way to estrange what I have internalised about teaching spaces.

Walking and Water Points

One way to think about space is by thinking about other spaces. It is easy to describe other spaces for writing pedagogy – the individual con-sultation, the workshop, the short course, the online platform. But that is not helpful for this project. Returning to Starke-Meyerring's (2014) point about doctoral practices and writing in particular as shrouded, the rest of this chapter tries to unshroud the circle, not by trying to capture it in a representational way as if to reveal reality, but in a way that defamiliarises pedagogic space by unthinking it.

I approach new spaces as a person who is walking, hoping to come back to the circle to lift, even for a moment, some of the shrouds. I try to unthink the circle by taking myself away from it to another experience of space, not just to make sense of what we have been doing, but to imagine other possibilities. There are no chairs, tables, doors or facilitators to pre-figure arrangements through the interpretive frame of classroom and pedagogy.

Reflection 3

I think of the paths on the Common. It's a flat pocket of land with busy roads on all four sides. It's a piece of land that has been fought for. It is criss-crossed daily, some taking a short cut to get to work, others with dogs, or looking for tadpoles, or flying a kite or model plane. I tell my friend that I love going there. She says she's always had a bad feeling about it, something about the trees. Pine trees. You can enter at any point, can't quite start in the middle though. Unless by drone? It's for wayfaring – on your way somewhere, part of the rhythm of the day. This city needs a project – we need a handful of symbolic places to give over, re-locate, traverse afresh. The Common is one of them.

While the Common is for everyone – ordinary, demarcated but not walled – it is a kind of buffer zone in what has always been contested space. Walking a dog, taking a short cut from work, taking part in a Park Run fitness campaign, waiting for tadpoles in spring. I follow an Instagram account that tracks changes in vegetation on the Common. Tiny star-like flowers have appeared on the edge of the puddles. They would have thrived before the Common was flattened to 'create a cricket pitch', says the ethnobotanist who runs the account. In precolonial times it provided grazing for herders. It has since been many things: a camp for troops during successive colonial occupations interested in securing the outpost at the Cape of Good Hope; a recreation ground where cricket and football matches were played; a public washing place when the pools filled up after the winter rains; a national monument to indigenous fynbos vegetation, and a site occupied by the 'Take back the Commons' movement in 2012. The caption for an aerial photograph of the Common[8] notes that 'The network of paths revealed by this photograph is hardly noticeable from the ground'.

The national botanical gardens, another walking space that I seek, is different. The garden needs a ticket, and it's expensive. Paths are more clearly demarcated.

Reflection 4

The walking itself brings new thought, movement. I'm drawn to the same route, turn left halfway up over the ford, follow signs to the gorge, pause in the shade at the fountain, then up, through the knotted trees, verticals, diagonals, horizontals in a fabulous, shaded tangle. That's my best part, but I don't stop there. Cross the road and keep on up into the mountain, aware that without thinking about it, I'm now out of the gardens and in the reserve. I pause where the paths cross, tune in to the small bubbles of conversation of others on the path. Different accents and languages, some of which I recognise. The sound of running water fades.

The fountain is a place to pause. Deleuze and Guattari (1987) use the image of the water point to explore the space of the nomad, emergence and the in-between.

> The water point is reached only in order to be left behind; every point is a relay and exists only as a relay. A path is always between two points, but the in-between has taken on all the consistency and enjoys both an autonomy and a direction of its own. The life of the nomad is the intermezzo. (Deleuze & Guattari, 1987: 380)

The points for water, dwelling, assembly etc. are known to the nomad but are always 'subordinate to the paths they determine', and to 'the trajectory that is mobilising them' (1987: 380). The water point is a moment in a pathway where travellers and things – animals, technologies, burdens, goods to be traded – intersect where there are stories, gossip, renewal, where formations coagulate and dissolve. Where water bottles are filled, stretching the dry skin. But resources cannot be taken for granted. The wells and streams may be dry. Like the burrows and rats in the quote at the beginning of this chapter, the water point is invested with multiple meanings made by the trajectories of the life forms that intersect there.

Water. There is too much or not enough in the Anthropocene. It falls on the land, seeps through to form vital groundwater and water points, surface tension constantly at work on many levels.

We try to channel it in drains and canals. Pipelines.

How do I write, asks Stephen King (2000). One word at a time. How do I walk? One step at a time. How do I breathe? In, out, one at a time. All involve a temporal unfolding in the body. Marijn Niewenhuis (2019: 50) reminds us in 'Ephemeral language: Communicating by breath' that 'the author's heart and mind dwell, quite literally, in the text' but that 'the reading and writing of academic text too often feels estranged, unfelt and instrumental [...] Success here, in the factory of ideas, is more than ever measured in the ability to disarm and neutralise the subversive potential of language'. I write (we write, they write?) in what might start as crazy gulps but end up as measured tones. The crazy gulps are not false starts. They constitute the thought even as it is left behind.

Through and Between

Back to the circlers. They write across multiple spaces. They pop up here and there. They are zig-zagging, seeking what they need to keep the momentum. My notes express anxiety. Who will come? Will the circle survive?

Reflection 5
Avril hasn't come for months. Last time I saw her, she arrived with a visiting academic who hardly said a word. They seemed to be comfortable, though we had an unusual session that day, sharing our experiences of the TurnItIn [plagiarism detection software] requirements. Now she is back again, saying 'I need to fall in love with my research again'.

Reflection 6
Eric is lost, angry, bouncing between people. Aditi suggests he come to the circle. He is looking for a supervisor. He needs to figure out how he got here. I suggest that he comes to the circle for a while. He comes three or four times. A year later I see him in the Arts building with a new supervisor... looks quite different, as if a burden has been shed.

There is no one place to begin, or to end.

Reflection 7

Naomi comes back six months after graduating. She says she'd have liked to have kept the continuity after graduation but didn't as Kit had come to one of the circles, and she doesn't feel comfortable (they work in the same unit). Kit never came back. I don't know why, don't need to know why.

Reflection 8

I saw Shandu in the mall the other day, we greeted warmly, she introduces me to her partner. 'I'm writing, but I've been delinquent from the writing group...' 'That's fine, as long as you keep moving ☺' I say.

The circle is changing even as it repeats itself. New people, new projects, new accents. It is alive, constantly morphing in relation to other spaces. It is part of an assemblage that makes and remakes itself, drawing new elements in as people, materials, tools change. It is a space of difference, not just in the literal sense of different disciplines or different pedagogy or different bodies. Knowledge will out as the new knowledge-makers zig-zag their way through the writing journey via burrows, watering holes, circuses.

I have travelled with different concepts to try and understand the circle and to imagine it differently as a space of becoming. The next chapter explores the methods that give shape to this journey.

Notes

(1) The idea of safe space emerged when I read about Marie Louise Pratt's notion of safe houses in her seminal paper on literacy, 'Arts of the contact zone' (1991: 40). See Chris Waugh (2019) for a deep look at the origins of safe space, its roots in both the LGBTQA student movement and feminist consciousness-raising groups of the 60s and 70s, how it has been weaponised in the neoliberal university, where 'safe spaces' becomes a proxy for 'woke' and 'cancel' cultures. Waugh argues for the ongoing usefulness of the term for the nurturing of what he calls subaltern counterpublics where the possibilities exist to 'create the vocabularies of resistance' (2019: 140).

(2) This poster had a short life. We replaced it with a more bold, abstract and urgent image that would appeal to postgraduates more than my homespun, cottagey image.

(3) Apartheid entrenched the categorisation of people in raced and ethnic terms as a pillar of the regime. The practice continues as institutions argue that there is still a need to 'see' and count 'race' if we are to introduce and evaluate policies to transform the university. There has long been a concern that if left undisturbed, student enrolments at the postgraduate level would continue along the lines of the past, advancing the interests of a knowledge elite – largely white and male, based at the historically white universities.

(4) See Jonathan Jansen (2003) for a description of the policy shift from post-apartheid massification to institutional mergers.

(5) These reflections are numbered to correspond with their order in this book rather than to signal a chronology of the reflections.

(6) The phenomenon of women's participation in writing groups is widely acknowledged. Agnes Bosanquet *et al.* (2014) in their chapter 'An Intimate Circle: Reflections on Writing as Women in Higher Education' describe their writing group at a research-intensive Australian university. They note that all five participants in the group designed to raise the profile of a teaching and learning unit are women, although this was not the original intention. Other groups such as described by Barbara Grant and Sally Knowles (2000) are designed for women in the academy and are underpinned by feminist pedagogy.

(7) Aditi wrote this reflection while she, Clement and I were working together on Chapter 7, "'I remember a few rogue popcorns...": Teaching for the Trace'. We were writing separately and together, separated by the pandemic, in Mauritius, Australia and South Africa respectively. Aditi started her 'I remember' entry with an exploration of the online circle she had facilitated the previous day.

(8) https://digitalcollections.lib.uct.ac.za/collection/islandora-16613, part of the Independent Newspapers Archive housed at the University of Cape Town. The photograph was taken because of concerns about urban 'encroachment' on the Common.

2 The Yellow Folders Draw Me In: Looking for the Trace

> I shall purloin no valuables, appropriate no ingenious
> formulations. But the rags, the refuse – these I will not inventory
> but allow, in the only way possible, to come into their own: by
> using them.

Walter Benjamin (1999: 460) The Arcades Project

This chapter explores the against the grain methods that I try out in this quest for the trace. I share my experience of tentatively entering the ragged yellow folders that are a haphazard record-of-sorts for the existence of the circle. Pausing on the yellow folders and some of the discarded written texts from the circle, the inquiry moves beyond my reconstructions and reflections in Chapter 1. These texts in the folders give a glimpse of the research interests of the postgraduate scholars in the circle. I peel back the process of writing and thinking about the folders and their contents to share the immersive, rhizomatic approach to writing that informs the method of this book. I describe what it is like to bump into things, including theory, that take off in new directions; to use other modes (a sketch) to enrich interpretation, and to experiment with form as in the way I arrange material in a collage without smothering it with interpretation. In foregrounding affect, which is significant before it finds form in language, I raise the importance of writing differently, at an oblique angle, as we 'forge connections to new ends' (Gibbs, 2015: 223).

Drawing Closer

The yellow buff folders keep me out.

Ashy flakes fall as I take the folders from the Spar carrier bag. The lining has perished.

I circle round them on the table, planning a line of approach, a way to draw them, and draw something out of them.

Drawing changes my relationship to the pile of folders. It alerts me to their materiality, to the torn folder, the crenelated paper plates, the sharp delicacy of the loose pages, to feeling the precarity of knowledge-making. They are no longer daunting, but alive. At any minute, this tower could

Figure 2.1 Sketch of the pile of yellow folders

collapse, scattering the pages. There would be no way to put them back as I know that the sheets of paper inside are unlikely to have been dated. The folders are curvy, they have different weightings. The pages are impossibly subtle in their textures and tones. The shadows are deep, sometimes warm, sometimes cold.

I am taken over. I feel as if I am 'participating in something like a visceral function, such as digestion or sweating, a function that is independent of the conscious will' (Berger, 2011: 149). With the displacement of words comes a change in subjectivity, from a person who writes but who is also drawing, not to freeze or capture, but to behold, to see afresh. I planned to start with a delicate ballpoint pen but chose instead a stubby indelible pen that could give more varied lines. It was what I had to hand.

Immersion

I arrange them in chronological order. One (the fattest) has 'Notes on WO (early)' handwritten on the cover. 2009, a gap, then there is one for each year: 2011, 2012, 2013, 2014, 2015, 2016, 2017. 2018 is missing.

It is an incomplete record of the existence of the Thursday Writers' circle. It stands for the period during which I was a facilitator, overlapping initially with Clement and later with Aditi. I know roughly what is inside. There are left-over two-pagers. The ones with comments have been given back to the person whose work is being discussed. There are also handouts on skills-builder activities as well as the forms that record participant details, which circlers complete at the end of the two hours together where they jot down their plans for the next week. These leftovers are loosely gathered in the yellow folders that now confront me. This is the surplus that wasn't used in the circle. How will I forge a creative link between the ongoing becoming of the journey, and the power of the destination? I need a method, a plan of sorts.

These yellow folders are traces of the material that has gathered around the circle. They are worn because I carried them around with me. Most folders have my handwritten notes scattered on the front cover. These notes are hooks for memory to take flight as I return years later to the folders for a different purpose. 2013 has five names set out in bullet points. Perhaps I forgot the participant details form on that day. There's also an email address for the student Max introduced in the previous chapter: the circle would not have been a safe space for him. The 2011 folder has ThINK in red ballpoint pen with the second part of the word, INK, underlined. It must have struck me as a good name for something. Reading it now, I enjoy it all over again. *Putting the 'ink' in 'think'*. It might be useful for the next workshop I am due to give on writing. The relationship between thinking and writing. I have always enjoyed the name of the writing programme at Queen Mary University London – ThinkingWriting – described by Teresa McConlogue, Sally Mitchell and Kelly Peake (2012). It carries no deficit connotations. The folder for 2012 has 'permanent head damage' scrawled in pencil. That's all. I must have heard this acronym for PhD for the first time. Another acronym that is circulating is Pull Him Down, a sceptical tall poppy reaction to the status that the PhD confers. The 2015 folder has some names – Kapoor, Joseph Nye – and book titles as we shared resources: 'Salsa dancing through the social sciences', 'Ethical quandaries in the social sciences', Hickey-Moodie, affect as method. There are also some phrases picked up from circlers that caught my ear at the time: 'write or die'; 'As simple as possible, as complex as necessary' (attributed to a lecturer in Sociology), and 'Piss on everyone's chips', a pithy phrase followed by my weak translation, 'burn your bridges'.

I am daunted by the chaos in the folders. How to make sense of them while doing justice to the complexity of the practices that they represent? For the first few years of the circle, we counted and set targets to justify strategic funding we had received from our faculty to bolster initiatives in support of postgraduate research writing. In my folder for the early years of the circle, there are over 40 pages of handwritten notes on foolscap paper, with sketches of who sat where at the table, and detailed notes of the rhetorical moves and key content words to represent the discussion at the table. This was a method of data-making used during my PhD to capture the flow of interaction. In a box in the bottom corner of one of the pages are research notes: 'What kind of space? How does it relate to AcLits?[1] Both the method of note-taking and the research questions reflect the concerns of my PhD. This folder also has a printout with the heading 'Notes on first joint writer circle on 2 March 2006 in the Writing Centre' typed up by Clement, the first person to facilitate the circle. We were bringing to our praxis what we thought we knew about rigour in research – the need to leave no stone unturned, to have a clear question to bring to the data, to treat the data systematically, to seek a neat correspondence between the events and their representation in the only artefact that seems to matter – the textual product – in a recognisable genre. We were trying to inaugurate the circle in a scholarly way.

Over time, Clement and I resisted formal evaluation of the circles. There was something different going on in the circle that we wanted to understand. I continued to use the casual system of filing, which is to accumulate yellow folders on my desk and then put them away in a cupboard when they are no longer in use. Stored on computers are the weekly emails sent out to the group every Tuesday to alert students to circle highlights from the previous week and announce Thursday's events. These could create a spine, a more reliable trace. They are not in the folders. Also absent from the folders are the reflections I used in the previous chapter, which I erratically jotted down after a circle when something felt important. These notes externalised the strong emotions and dilemmas that arose from being facilitator of the circle. These all provide substantive written materiality. But the expanded archive – the wider and deeper archive that Bowker (2005, 2010) writes of – is about more than writtenness. It's about wayfaring, feelings, memory.

I am not sure how to move forward. Deep inside me is a refusal to enter the life of this circle armed with a pre-ordained method that would break its delicate power. And my chaotic archive is ragged and incomplete. Can I trust it?

Synchronicity and the Trace

Thoughts about how to approach the lifeworld of the circle through this discarded material take a different form as I immerse myself in the folders. I open the folder on top of the pile and there is a copy of a research proposal with this cover page:

To: Dr Neville Alexander

Subject: Research Proposal

Proposed Topic: To establish whether Ubuntu Philosophy[2] is taught in the classroom as part of the Environmental Education or Life Orientation in schools around Cape Town.

The writer is an Honours student whose name I have forgotten. The proposal is addressed to the student's supervisor, Neville Alexander, a pioneering South African language activist and scholar. He is dead now. The loss washes over me, but also the found. There is a building on campus recently named after him, acknowledging the reach of his language and literacy work.

Chance takes me to a pile of inscribed paper plates wedged in the folder for 2012. We wrote on these at the end of the final circle for the year in November 2012. I had brought a celebratory cake, hence the paper plates. At the end of the circle, we all wrote down our plans for the following year. On the spur of the moment, I decided to use the paper plates rather than the usual A4 foolscap or A5 notebook that can be bought in a stationery shop. The affordance of the circular 'page' has been used in different ways by those present. The one in Figure 2.2 (is it made by Estella, that beautiful handwriting?) has been written in a spiral.

I read, turning the plate so I don't need to read upside down. Starting in the middle,

> *'I will make a plan so I don't have to be part of someone else's plan! (Neville Alexander). Next year I plan to have written my first draft and I plan to be in a position ...'*

There is Neville Alexander's name again.

How did it get there? I must have shared an anecdote about a student in a postgraduate course, who had quoted Neville's advice about making a plan before you are part of someone else's plan. This must have travelled into the circle at some stage, reappearing when I asked circlers to write about their 'next' – what they hoped for in the following year.

How can it be that I have just been writing about him and then I read his name in the middle of the spiral on the paper plate? I wasn't looking for it. It found me.

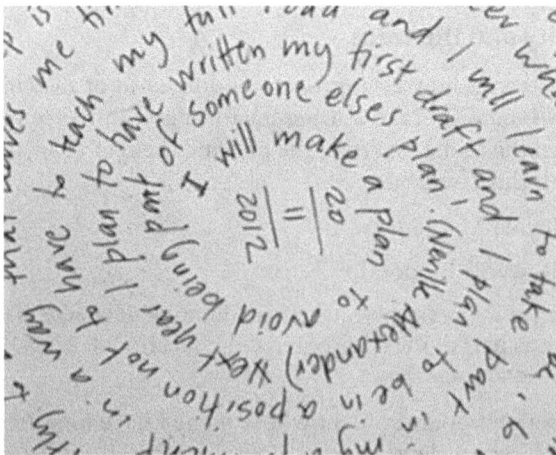

Figure 2.2 'I will make a plan...' Plans for next year written on a paper plate at end-of-year gathering

Synchronicity – where internal and external reality coincide. A zone of contact. A form of surface tension. Do these chance-saturated material flows and encounters have a place in the academy? We are compelled to cover our tracks and delete this back stuff when we write arguments in journal articles in which we have to straighten the line and turn a blind eye to the traces by which we have come to know things. The structure of the traditional positivist research article – Introduction, methods, results, analysis, discussion – requires us to align question/hypothesis, theory, method in a display of objectivity *after* the doing of our research. What happens if you come to the theory late? The situated literacy practices of doing research differ so substantially from the final, cleaned up, sanitised, commodified published product that it is a challenge for researchers to keep faith with the process.

Another meaningful coincidence. While searching my DropBox archive to save the photograph of the spiral on the paper plate, I bump into a forgotten text, a review of Geoffrey Bowker's (2005) *Memory Practices in the Sciences*. The review by Claire Waterton (2007) picks up on the idea of the 'mnemonic deep', which is Bowker's phrase for how memory and time work to (skimming the pdf review) 'reveal the past not as a series of sequential events occurring in the world, but as the outcome of a process of creating, making marks, leaving traces, and, in the case of natural scientists, carrying out an active editing of these traces' (2007: 180). I am trying not to edit as I read/write/bump into/glance at/glance off the traces left by these writers. Synchronicity brings Bowker's ideas about archives back, just when I am ready to receive them.

I enter the river of thinking–reading–writing where I am part of the thought flow, where ideas and associations may spark, seemingly at random, to feel what it is like for something new to come into being. In conventional qualitative research, one would edit out the sparking, associations, serendipity, in favour of neat alignment between question and answer within the bounds of thematic ringfencing to avoid leakage, pollution, contamination, mess.

Traces. The trace archive. Bowker's argument about the quest for the trace archive makes more sense as I am living the process. The idea of the trace archive and how it might inform this exploration of the circle as a problem space gathers momentum. The scraps from the folders may or may not tell us anything about the interface between what Bowker (2005, 2010), borrowing from Derrida, calls the jussive archive and the more elusive trace archive. This is another zone of contact. The jussive archive is about what is permissible and generalisable, about the 'shoulds', which is what most thesis writing guides give us. They give us templates, certainties, recipes. But these often hide the accumulated traces with which they are in a necessary relationship. The trace archive is experiential, *laissez-faire* and embodied. It is open to experimental 'what if?' work which invites moods that are playful, sombre, joyful, baffled. It is not bound by the logics of generalisability and objectivity. 'We do not need another description of formal archives' writes Bowker (2010: 213). No, there are enough 'how to' templates around that we writers mis-recognise. The internet is freighted with them. But like fast foods, they tend to leave us hungry because they do not speak to the power dynamics and entangled materiality of people, projects, time and place.

Synchronicity again. Michael Taussig's *The Corn Wolf* (2015) appears in my peripheral vision, sent to me by a friend. It is a passionate inquiry into the false separation between anthropological fieldwork and what he calls 'writingwork' (2015: 2). He argues that the researcher's fieldnotes, with all their richness, cannot be seen as 'mere stepping stones to the polished end-product of a book or article:

> This is not a plea for exact reproduction of the fieldwork notebook but rather a plea for following its furtive forms and mix of private and public in what can only be called, as in cinema, a 'dissolve' or 'fade out' that captures ephemeral realities, the check and bluff of life. (2015: 76)

It matters to take the 'furtive forms' a stage further towards the product. The commodification of writing does not need to be inscribed again. We need the check and bluff, sleight of hand, bold darts, lines of flight.

The 2016 Folder: A Collage

Pick a folder: 2016. 2015 and 2016 were momentous for the University and for higher education nationally. The #RhodesMustFall protests in 2015 began at UCT over coloniality, being and belonging and were followed by the year of #FeesMustFall, with momentum from the University of Witwatersrand where the focus was more on financial exclusion. There were times when the University was closed when all classes and regular activities were suspended.

For this chapter, I shall focus on the 2016 folder as that was a particularly challenging year. The papers don't seem to be in any chronological order, though my usual practice was to add the most recent texts to the top of the pile. There is a mixture of the notional two pages – a variety of process texts including draft research questions, interview schedules, summaries of books – that the circlers have brought for airing. There is a flyer for a literacy project that is looking for support. There are materials used as skills builders – on writing abstracts, good titles, print-outs of entries from Pat Thomson's 'Patter' wonderful blog[3] on academic writing. Some sessions were used to run through presentations for conferences or for job interviews. There is no textual trace in the folders for these texts. The material to hand is the bits that were left over, not used by the people in the room on the day.

There are lots of the writer circle participant details forms, one for every gathering (see Figure 2.3). The largest has 13 attendants and the

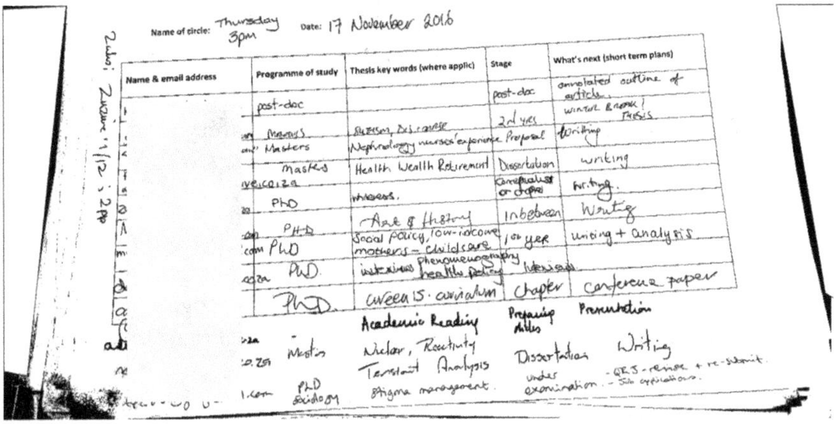

Name of circle: Thursday 3pm Date: 17 November 2016

Name & email address	Programme of study	Thesis key words (where applic)	Stage	What's next (short term plans)
	post-doc		post-doc	annotated outline of article.
	Masters		2nd yrs	winter break! Thesis
	Masters	Nephrology nurses' experience	Proposal	Writing
	masters	Health Wealth Retirement	Dissertation	writing
	PhD	whiteness.		writing.
	PHD	Art & History	Inbetween	Writing
	PhD	Social Policy, low-income mothers – childcare	1st year	writing + analysis
	PhD	interviews Phenomenography health policy		
	PhD.	careers · curriculum	Chapter	conference paper
		Academic Reading	Preparing slides	Presentation
	Masters	Nuclear, Reactivity Transient Analysis	Dissertation	Writing
	PhD Sociology	Stigma management.	under examination.	– revise + re-submit.

Figure 2.3 Participant details form for one of the biggest circles in 2016

smallest has three: 2016 was no exception. The circle waxes and wanes. It breathes in and out.

For the participant details form for the largest group, names and email addresses have been removed. This is the standard form we were using at the time. The column 'name of circle' denotes that this was just one of many circles, some tied to disciplines and projects. The Thursday circle was the most freewheeling one. It was a large group on that day, with postgraduates with very different disciplinary backgrounds and projects. 'Health, wealth, retirement' and 'whiteness' are adjacent in the thesis key words column. The students doing 'Art and History' and 'Nuclear, reactivity, analysis' popped into the circle briefly after being told about it on a research development course in the suite of postgraduate offerings from my unit, before moving on to spaces more likely to meet their needs at the time. People interpret 'Stage' very differently, some using the linear staging of the trajectory of the thesis candidature and beyond ('under examination' and 'post-doc'), others give the micro-task ('preparing slides'). Under 'What's next?' several simply state 'writing' while others are more specific. These forms are filled in at the end of the circle before everyone leaves, as a ritual, and are seldom looked at. We facilitators assume that students will notice that they are stuck if they keep saying the same thing for many months.

Below is a collage of some of the key identifiers – titles and/or first few lines of the texts in the folder. These are extracted from the extra copies of the two pages under discussion on the day. They are arranged as an unsystematic skim across the surface of the texts left behind. A skim of this collage will give a taste of some of the knowledge projects that we read over six months.[4] There is a range of work-in-progress texts: some such as interview schedules, summaries or notes on how a concept was developed through NVivo coding, are unlikely to appear in the final thesis or article. There are several introductions. What do not appear here are draft conference presentations and dry-runs for job interviews – fairly common for the circlers who stayed on after thesis completion.

- **Working title:** Distorting discourses of safety and security: Interactions between waste pickers and agents of formal social control on the streets of Cape Town.

- Reflexivity
  Three months after registering to do a PhD a friend sent me a 'Great big story' video of an American obstetrician investigation the 500% increase in the rate of caesarean sections in just one generation of mothers.

- **SYNOPSIS**
  Healthcare in South Africa is undergoing significant changes as it seeks to address a system characterised by inequalities between public and privately funded health service.

- **An Exploration into Nephrology Nurses' Experiences of Caring for Dying Patients with End Stage Kidney Disease Following Withdrawal of Dialysis**

- Teaching practices to empower the "voiceless"
  Paulo Freire's philosophy of critical literacy (1970) uses education to shape the person and society with hope and autonomy.

- MAIN RESEARCH QUESTIONS
  What are the (emotional) negotiations shaping pathways through pregnancy for women, men and couples and how do these shape the narratives, experiences and meanings of childbirth?

- **Developing the concept of motivation as a dimension of agency based on the data guided by Bazeley (2013: Chapter 8).**

- Creche facilitator/principal interview schedule

  (1) Is your creche independent or does it receive some state support?
  (2) How would you describe the experience of caring for so many children who all come from different households and backgrounds, all raised differently?

- Project design for the RDR strategy that aims to transform the academy to be more representative of the demographics of the South African population

The concerns of the world system are present in these scraps, with an accent from the global south. Transforming the academy, public vs private funding, reflexivity, emancipation and agency of people in marginal employment, failing healthcare, death and dying, inequality, diversity. Underneath the titles, doing the fieldwork for these projects was often challenging: accompanying waste-pickers on their rounds of the streets; running literacy classes for vendors of *The Big Issue* (a monthly magazine sold by marginalised and unemployed adults at traffic intersections); joining a group of women in informal employment in townships when the researcher's accent marked her as an 'outsider'; being a professional alongside a patient who is dying because of funding cuts. All this in a precarious university, where the nature of knowledge-making is both contested and energised against the background of the #RMF and #FMF protests. The politics and intensity are masked in the titles and the strips of writing above.

Not everyone did finish their thesis. One student withdrew when policy governing the training of nurses changed, delivering a blow to her project. Another withdrew when it became clear that she could be a more effective literacy activist by starting a sewing non-governmental organisation (NGO) with unemployed women. The NGO is thriving. One deregistered as a distance candidate at an overseas university while fighting for study leave from a demanding job as a senior administrator.

There are several handouts on skills-builders. These seem to be at odds with the gravity of the knowledge projects that students were undertaking:

From predator to pet: Three techniques for taming your writing project

Levels of analysis in academic writing

Art of the **TITLE**

I close the 2016 folder, feeling the joy and the weight and the richness that came with the Thursday circle.

The yellow folders give us a glimpse of the traces, tracks, footprints of life in the circle. They can be experienced by bringing them alive through writing about them. And I am trying to learn to write differently.

Writing as a Mode of Inquiry

In this chapter so far, there are moments when my writing tries to keep up with thinking, moments when images come to the rescue, and moments when things are gathered and laid out, with minimal interpretation. I try to translate the process of discovery of found objects loosely bound in folders, and the memories that they invoke, into an experience to share with the reader that meets the academic knowledge-making project half-way. This is done to explore the interface between subjective and objective, inside and outside, formal and informal ways of knowing.

It slowly becomes clear to me that an important part of the method guiding this ethnographic deep dive is that I need to grasp the potentials of writing differently. This desire to write differently is in part because of the nature of the Thursday circle. In the previous chapter, I described the circle as a brave space (Arao & Clemens, 2013) rather than a safe space. It is a space offset from the mainstream, a two-way portal between the formal and trace archives, in an osmotic relationship between the two, where students will pause at the water point in the flux of becoming. The knowledge-making journey opens us to registers of feeling and we bring that vulnerability to the circle. As facilitators, we are open to surprise, often out of our depths, feeling our way. As a researcher, uncertainty is important in what and how I see, remember, hope and fear.

This openness to feeling is given form in the concept of affect[5] and in affect theory, following Deleuze and Guattari in its formulation as intensities that are becomings in relation to the other, in all forms – human, material, abstract (Deleuze & Guattari, 1987). Understood as pre-personal intensity, affect can be productive as an indicator of our commitments to how we are showing up in the world. It is 'the body's way of preparing us for action' (Shouse, 2005). For Brian Massumi (2015), affect is political in that it invites us to think about change through the body's sensory modes of response and resistance to power relations under neoliberal capitalism before these responses are socially determined. Affect is significant before it finds form in language and so it cannot be fully realised in language (Massumi, 2015). We can try to name and capture and explain feelings associated with laughter, shame, procrastination, the joy of flow, but more important than this capturing, is staying with feeling in its complexity, recognising that it can't all be put into words. Arguing for affect as 'process oriented exploration' (2015: xi) Massumi asks:

> What would an objective or general approach bring to the singular qualities of life that compose its affective dimension? Stilling. Dullening. Dead disciplinary reckoning. The aim is not to convince with claims of validity, but rather to convey something of the vivacity of the topic. (2015: viii)

Conveying something of the life of the topic involves re-thinking the relationship between the written language and knowledge-making. This opens the door to immersive approaches that disrupt 'the tripartite division between the field of reality (the world) and a field of representation (the book) and the field of subjectivity (the author). Rather, an assemblage establishes connections between certain multiplicities drawn from each of these orders' (Deleuze & Guattari, 1987: 25). Approaching the field through writing in this rhizomatic way to make new connections, I am exploring the contours of this tripartite division to create assemblages – collections of stuff – that enable us to see them afresh.

A feature of this assemblage writing is to understand and celebrate writing as an 'active ambiguous and slippery phenomenon that will inevitably launch the writing subject into unexpected situations – both positive and negative' (Lykke *et al.*, 2014: 3). They embrace writing as a mode of inquiry for developing feminist and intersectional methodologies which strive for ethical ways of unfolding the relationship between the researcher I and the object of research across signifiers of class, race, gender, nationality, sexuality. This always involves some degree of self-writing (Braidotti, 2014), whether explicit or not.

Taking my cue from literacy theorists who step back from a reification of the text and bring Deleuzian rhizomatic thinking to literacy, for this study I hope to create that feeling of jumping straight in, suspending the prescriptions about what makes good writing, to embrace the becoming. As Leander and Boldt (2012: 41) argue, 'Literacy *is* unbounded'. By trying to hold it down, and failing to travel with it, we risk missing out on how it can spill and flow. Rhizomatic approaches ask us to jump in in the middle, yet I know, and we all know, though we may forget, that there is a laying down, a sedimentation, that structures our horizons around what is possible. We cannot ignore this. This imaginary of what we feel academic language *should* look like, what in the next chapter I explore as divine discourse (Cadman, 2003) and the god view (Haraway, 1988), casts a long shadow over knowledge-making.

Deleuze and Guattari (1987) invite an unruly approach to language, allowing the spill and flow, in an invitation to do rhizomatic inquiry that celebrates a different view of language as emergent, that 'spreads like a patch of oil' as a countermove to the focus in linguistics on universals and stable forms:

> There is no language in itself, nor are there any linguistic universals, only a theory of dialects, patois, slangs, and specialized languages. [...]. There is no mother tongue, only a power takeover by a dominant language within a political multiplicity. Language stabilizes around a parish, a bishopric, a capital. It forms a bulb. It evolves by subterranean stems and flows, along river valleys or train tracks; it spreads like a patch of oil. (Deleuze & Guattari 1987: 7)

Taking this idea of language to writing, presumably writing too 'forms a bulb' as it evolves along the channels and pathways where bodies move. It is this movement – processual unfolding – that I am interested in.

I have always been drawn to views of language and literacy as emergent, creative, imperfect, as striving for something more than what we are handed down. My desire may be shaped by years of teaching writing in this postcolonial world where there is always a surplus – something more that is going on that asks for our attention. Dissonance, violence, tenderness crowd in on language. In Deleuze and Guattari's (1987) writing together, it feels as if they are trying to expand the notion of not just writing, but also reading. Frustrating and illuminating in equal parts, it's a crazy ride that traverses interfaces seemingly at random. They explore ideas through refracted, splintered, flowing prose that is close to the pulse of thought. It sometimes feels like stream of consciousness writing with no concern to make it legible for the reader. But in-between it is sonorous and dignified. It is important because it draws attention to the complex relationship between language and representation. But I also know that it is very hard to teach this approach as pedagogy or method. It has to be lived, in the reading and the writing.

Anna Gibbs (2015) takes processual approaches to writing further by explaining how affective research writing can be thought of as a mode of inquiry, a politics and practice for both critique and affirmation. For Gibbs, affective research writing as 'the experimental and productive forging of connection to new ends, rather than the analytical disassembling of a machine in order to see how it works' (2015: 223). In a process parallel to engaging with our espoused methodologies, many scholars become aware of the way writing has a life of its own as it plunges us into dialogue with different voices – of theorists, participants in the research process, the voice of scientific objectivity – as it constantly interrupts itself while trying to maintain coherence. For Gibbs (2005), this interrelationship between writing and thinking suggests the possibility that writing can also be a mode of inquiry in its own right – 'a way of writing for which there is no blueprint and which must be constantly invented anew in the face of the singular problems that arise in the course of engagement with what is researched'. But writing is not a 'methodological "tool" in any simple sense. It is, rather, a process, implicitly dialogical, in conversation with the world, with other writing, and, reflexively, with itself' (2015: 3). In the 2015 article, Gibbs elaborates on aspects of this processual, dialogic writing: attunement, resonance and rhythm. At the heart of the process is subjectivity in motion – subjectivity that 'risks itself':

> Writing is inevitably a process in which subjectivity continually risks itself, finds itself, loses itself, and remakes itself in its dialogic relations with the world to which it attunes. If affective attunement is the first task of writing, the second is affective resonance, achieved when writing finds the form adequate to which it describes. (2015: 227)

Affective attunement echoes Braidotti's (2014) view of writing as 'the visualization of ethical relationality' described in the Introduction. The search for resonance – finding the most apt form to communicate this relationality – is animated by rhythm. Gibbs (2015) shows how, in a time when corporatisation of the university coincides with the dominance of communication patterns underpinned by the algorithm, rhythm offers forms of writing that are closer to orality and to poetry: in this mode of writing, subjectivity is fluid, 'finding and losing itself' in relationship to the world it is sharing with readers. This is as true for researchers who work with affect as it is for the postgraduate students who come to the circle. By consciously choosing writing as a method that does not position itself at a clear critical distance, 'pretending the objectivity and the 20/20 vision of hindsight which enables the forms of judgement characterising work in the mode of critique' (2015: 13–14), the writer takes a risk. It is a politics of both critique[6] and affirmation of potential. Perhaps the politics and the critique also lie in my refusal to adopt a consistent, codified approach to representation, or to adopt a single methodology.

There are interesting links to be made between processual approaches to writing and semiotic activity beyond writing. Using drawings or modes other than written language in this inquiry creates opportunities to explore my long-held interest in the potentially transformative uses of multimodal pedagogy in the teaching of writing.[7] For example, the moment of drawing the folders in the current chapter is what Denise Newfield (2014) calls a 'transmodal moment' in a chain of semiosis – a moment of pause, or punctuation in Gunther Kress's terms, in the movement across texts, where it is possible to shift emphasis for a brief period. To tie a knot in the string. These allow for 'shifts in materiality, medium, genre as well as meaning, orientation, disposition, subjectivity, identity and affect' (2014: 6). These transmodal moments invite different forms, aesthetics and responses.

But I am also inevitably involved with representation. There is no one approach that can live up to the tensions, dilemmas and delights of trying to bring the writers' circle to life for others. In the dialogical sense envisaged by Gibbs, I have to describe the circle, and be in conversation with the world, in ways that others will recognise. So I swerve between an experimental, emergent approach and what looks like more conventional qualitative analysis which is preoccupied with concerns about reliability and replicability, deemed to be achieved through objectivity. These concerns come from being in the shadow of positivist research. At times I am less interested in faithful recreations of the life of the circle than in creating new descriptions, that become open-ended 'events' to help us think differently about how things might be in the future. This concept of event as a becoming rather than as recognisable shape, with fixed coordinates in time and space, comes from Deleuze (2004). This is discussed more fully in Chapter 6 where I am more explicit about the research interview as an event as something that is always happening 'in the middle'. The relationality of the interview as Deleuzian event doesn't try to bracket or hold the event still, but to explore it for its rich potential, trying to feel the moment. Because of the internal structure and complexity of events, we are asked to think about time differently – more Aeon (lived-in time) than Chronos (measured, chronological time). This way of thinking about the event 'highlights the momentary uniqueness of the nexus of forces' (Stagoll, 2005: 90). This is a departure from mainstream Literacy Studies, where an event would be seen as an instance of practice, around which spatial and temporal boundaries can be drawn.

This chapter has shown the assemblage-writing approach that I use as a method animated by subjectivity to 'situate us amongst things'

(Meschonnic (2011) in Gibbs, 2015). The chapters that follow widen and deepen the concerns raised in this chapter, with a combination of anecdote and reflections that bring the circle alive, and new inquiries, particularly in Chapter 3, in a home 'experiment' with surface tension; Chapter 4, in a drawing of laughter as concept and a workshop on concepts in the thought flow; Chapter 6, retrospective interviews with Kay, Siwela and Tia, and Chapter 7, memory work with Clement and Aditi, written slowly over an extended period.

Silencing or ignoring the trace does violence to the knowledge-making project. Bringing concerns for social justice to writing and knowledge-making requires us to try to find ways to value the stuff that is left behind – the affect, materialities, presence and absence, refusals and moments of yielding. This requires an immersion in the sights and sounds of the circle and what it is touching on. Exploring writing as a mode of inquiry can help to bring the trace into view.

A sense of urgency is pushing me to look at the domain of the conventional written product – the destination that is typically envisaged at the end of the process, where the product settles in the formal archive. I think of the circle as a portal between trace and formal archives. In prioritising the trace, I cannot ignore the formal archive. I do this in the next chapter by returning to surface tension as a relational idea that holds together elements in contact. It is a concept-in-action that makes it possible to think about *both* trace *and* formal archives.

Notes

(1) Academic Literacies, the field I am invested in as a teacher/researcher interested in academic writing (see Introduction).

(2) The notion of ubuntu expresses the desire to identify an Africa-centred relational philosophy that is opposed to a colonial ethic founded on competition, individual rights and separateness. The expression 'I am because we are, and since we are, therefore I am' is attributed to philosopher of religion John Mbiti and the sayings *Motho ke motho ka batho babang* and *umntu ngumntu ngabantu* (a person is a person through other people) appear widely in public discourse. It is relatively easy to define, but more important is to ask what the idea of ubuntu *does*. See Precious Simba's PhD (2021), 'A Feminist Critique of Ubuntu: Implications for Citizenship Education in Zimbabwe' for a critical analysis, and Kate Cadman (2014) for a discussion of ubuntu in relation to knowledge-making in the global south.

(3) Pat Thomson's blog *Patter* is at https://patthomson.net/

(4) The 2016 folder is for the second semester of the year. I was on sabbatical leave in the first semester.

(5) Collections such as *The Affect Theory Reader* (Melissa Gregg & Gregory Seigworth, 2010) and *Affective Methodologies* (Britta Timm Knudsen & Carsten Stage, 2015) give a sense of the relevance and debates in what has been called 'the affective turn' (Patricia Ticineto Clough & Jean Halley, 2007).

(6) Here Anna Gibbs departs from Massumi, who sees working with affect as only about 'and' – affirmation – rather than critique.

(7) See the extensive work of Gunther Kress, Pippa Stein, Denise Newfield and Arlene Archer in this field.

3 Surface Tension: Writing in the Shadow of the God View

I had trained myself to be like them. And often I succeeded: it seemed to me that I had mastered words to the point of sweeping away forever the contradictions of being in the world, the surge of emotions, the breathless speech. In short, I now knew a method of speaking and writing that – by means of a refined vocabulary, stately and thoughtful pacing, a determined arrangement of arguments, and a formal orderliness that wasn't supposed to fail – sought to annihilate the interlocutor to the point where he lost the will to object.

Elena Ferrante (2014: vol. 3: 30) Those who leave and those who stay.
The Neapolitan Novels

If there's one thing I know it's that writing comes out of tension, tension between what's inside and what's outside. Surface tension, isn't that the phrase – actually that's not a bad title, is it?

Rachel Cusk (2014: 47) *Outline*

The formal archive is foregrounded in this chapter, with the focus on how it casts a shadow on the process of writing in the way it enacts the god view. The god view – what Donna Haraway calls the god trick, because it functions like magic – is the imaginary that academic discourse and its expression in writing is about achieving a disembodied, omniscient position of objectivity. From this vantage point one can look down and make sense of the world by means of generalisations buttressed by theory and a measured style. I explore aspects of knowledge-making and discourse, arguing for a view of theory as a verb, as action, rather than as something that pre-exists, that we find and then own. Illustrations from the circle will illuminate moments where circle participants have grappled with the tension at the interface between the trace and formal archives, weighing up what counts as rigour, which sources to trust, what styles might work.

Then I expand on the idea of surface tension as a form of conceptual interference at the interface between formal and trace archives, working with the notion of surface tension as a theoretical project 'to arrive at a transformational matrix of concepts apt to continue the open-ended journey of thinking-feeling life's processual qualities' (Massumi, 2015: xi). I describe how the concept of surface tension emerged as an idea that is always in play, that can foreground the flickering, shifting realities associated with the circle, and in the process, re-size the dominant view of academic writing - what Kate Cadman calls divine discourse (2003). As a form of interference, surface tension is a doing rather than a thing.

Two Stories from the Interface

The two stories that follow have been reconstructed from the circle. They illustrate the notion of the portal between archives and lead me to explore surface tension, the concept-in-action that plays out across this book. While the circle holds its shape but keeps moving as people and projects change, it remains in touch with the imagined solidity of the formal archive. There are moments of porousness as the archives interact.

> *In the early days of the circle*, Ellen shares a problem with us. She is writing about a sociolinguistic phenomenon in urban townships and has been using a well-known framework to analyse interaction. The theory does not travel well. We listen as Ellen shares what she is seeing, how the data doesn't fit the assumptions in the model. Vere suggests a new term, a lexical hybrid of more settled concepts in the model, and it resonates. It becomes a conceptual contribution in Ellen's thesis, with a footnote acknowledging Vere and the Thursday circle.

For Ellen, the circle helps to solve a dilemma. The theory with its sociolinguistic framework from the global north does not fit what she is finding out. A neologism offered by someone in the circle makes sense, and she runs with it and it becomes a key part of her findings. She acknowledges the provenance of the term in the thesis, but the conventions of the thesis restrict this to a footnote. Years later, in following through with the ethics process for this book, we discuss her discomfort with how she had attributed the concept and agree that being uncomfortable about knowledge-making isn't a bad thing. It's just that those discomforts are generally not aired in the formal archive.

> *Elizabeth is in the final months* of her PhD. She brings the first two pages of her introduction to the circle, with a specific request: she wants to use an image on the first page to catch the reader's attention and give her thesis more life. She wants to use the image to illustrate her chosen methodology, phenomenology. It is a cartoon-like illustration of the parable of the blind men and the elephant. Never having seen an elephant, they imagine and learn what the elephant is like by touching it. Each blind man feels a different part of the elephant's body, but only one part, such as the trunk or the side. When they get together to describe the elephant based on their limited experiences, they realise that although they have all touched the same creature, they come away with different conclusions about what the creature is like. After a lengthy discussion, we dissuade her from using it. It is too risky.

Elizabeth wants to innovate – to find a different way to introduce her study with an image. But we hold her back in the circle and persuade her otherwise. It is not so much the risk of starting the thesis with an image, but the tone of the image that feels wrong to us. Have we internalised the voice of the formal archive?

The two stories illustrate the dynamics of the circle in knowledge-making. These are stories about the weight of theory and style. We can't ignore the expectation and history that comes with the conventions of research writing. While the circle is like a water point – a place of emergence and flux where the trace lives – it is proximate to, and arguably exists *because of*, the imaginary of academic writing as a style that once mastered, in the words of novelist Elena Ferrante above, 'annihilates' the reader into submission. This is a bleak view. Through the circle, it is possible to imagine a different way of doing research writing where the trace and the formal archive mingle at a portal. Movement at this portal is not uni-directional: it goes both ways, but the pull towards the products of the formal archive is strong. Ellen's openness to innovation is affirmed; Elizabeth's is not, though her desire to innovate is welcomed.

The Knowledge Supermarket

The dominant image of scientific knowledge was vividly brought home to postgraduate scholars in a writing workshop at which some of the Thursday circle participants were present. In a round table discussion on knowledge-making in challenging contexts, my physicist colleague Saalih Allie, a facilitator at the workshop, emphasised the importance of writing along the way, as a counterpoint to the sanitised final product: 'It's like going to the supermarket, and there at the meat counter are your mince, your chicken wings, neatly packed and priced, but what we don't see is the abattoir. The blood, the pain, the messiness of the making', he said.

His comment is a sharp reminder of the shadow side of knowledge-making. It draws attention to how the supermarket hides the slaughterhouse. Neatly packaged journal articles arrive like chicken wings on the counter to be consumed but we know little about their provenance. The archive is a curation that is problematic as while appearing to be universal it hides profound blind spots, inadequacies and inequalities.

An extreme version of divine discourse is this description of scientific communication as 'faceless and passionless', written by a professor of physics quoted in Peter Elbow (1991):

> Scientific communication is faceless and passionless by design. Data and conclusions stand bare and unadorned, so they can be evaluated for what they are without prejudice or emotion. This kind of impersonal communication has helped science achieve the status of public knowledge, a coinage of truth with international currency. (Raymo (1989) in Elbow, 1991: 142)

The phrase 'coinage of truth' is apt given the commodification of knowledge in the academy. But scientific communication is not one thing. We are held captive by an imaginary of a mode of knowing and saying, something up there that pre-exists hovering above the mess and busy-ness of coming and going, failed projects, apologies, hopes and dreams. This god view is imagined as giving us panoptic objectivity as we borrow authority from others. And in the Anglosphere it comes wrapped in the English language in ways that make it difficult to imagine an alternative.

A particular kind of text written in the genre of the research article plays a central organising role in the now crowded, but infinitely digitally elastic, formal archive ('everybody listen now') of the academy. The research article has a characteristic shape (Introduction, Method, Results and Discussion) that Swales (2004) refers to as the RA (Research Article). This form achieves certain rhetorical moves that are based on positivist science but have a bearing on journal articles across the disciplines in which qualitative empirical research is done. The RA model is bolstered by the Anglocentric style that is valued in much of the academy – C-B-S: clarity, brevity, sincerity (Barnard, 2014). This style expresses a discursive value system that assumes that any ambiguity in the argument needs to be closed down. If ambiguity is the enemy, the inability to achieve this coherence on the reader's terms is seen as a sign of failure and deficit. Together the RA model of knowledge structure and CBS style extend beyond the research article to influence all scientific communication, including the writing of postgraduate research degrees. As Swales notes (2004: 107), the assumption that an empirical PhD will follow this format is often put forward in advice manuals and guides.

I was exposed to the power of style and how it affects reception as Aditi's supervisor. Her language and educational history meant that she could draw on Hindi, French and Creole in crafting her research writing in English. At some point she tried to switch from a more exploratory Francophone style that seemed to value keeping the complexity going as long as possible. This was the style in which I had first read her work as she brought her disciplinary background in literary studies and rhetoric to language and literacy studies. She said that when writing in French, being sparse and to the point was considered condescending to the reader and explained the convention of ending an academic text with 'en guise de conclusion' – by way of conclusion. As a supervisor, I was uncomfortable with her new stripped-down C-B-S style with its short sentences, preferring the richness of her earlier style, which sounded more 'scholarly' and more 'coherent' to my ears.

We know that getting the form or style more-or-less right does not comprise success if success is measured as getting one's work published in a way that counts in prominent accredited journals with high citation factors. Jan Blommaert's work (2005) on the relationship between form and function in written text shows powerfully how texts often don't travel well. In movement between sites, they hold their form, but not their meaning, as they move across geopolitical spaces that are not neutral. A text that works in the periphery could be found lacking in the Anglophone publishing centre but the 'evaluative regimes' of publishing (Lillis, 2017) would seldom turn that relationship on its head. The reference point for quality remains in the global north, underpinned by normative notions of what is correct and authoritative in the production of written research. The interaction between bibliometric measures and the requirement to publish in English amplifies the orthodoxies that guard the process of writing and publication. In South African higher education these trends are intensified by the unusual practice of financially rewarding individuals directly for research outputs, particularly theses and articles in accredited journals, though not all institutions (including my own) have taken this up (Cloete & Mouton, 2015). It seems as if smaller and smaller parcels of knowledge get packaged ever more safely so in the end, what counts as a contribution to knowledge is miniscule and backward looking. The dangers of this 'salami slicing' are noted in a 2005 Editorial in the journal *Nature Materials* (vol. 4 (1), see nature.com/naturematerials). The washback from these time-is-money approaches to knowledge is pervasive and restrictive for postgraduate thesis writers: there is less time and space to make data differently, to slow down and think, as postgraduates are simultaneously publishing short articles while working on extended PhD processes where knowledge-making does not feel stable or predictable. And recipes for writing conventions get more and more dogmatic.

Exploring Alternatives

It is misleading to generalise too broadly about research writing conventions of the formal archive because there are many exceptions and hidden histories even within canonical western science.[1] A remarkable example of doing things differently is the 'Blackawton Bees' paper in *Biology Letters* (4 January 2011). The 'author', P.S. Blackawton *et al.*, is a pseudonym for a class of 11-year-olds from a primary school in Blackawton in Devon in the UK, who under the guidance of their teacher, ran experiments to test the colour sense of bees. The paper includes reproductions of the children's hand-drawn diagrams. In the Discussion section of the paper they write: 'This experiment is important because as far as we know, no-one in history (including adults) has done this experiment before' (2011: 4). While conforming to the overall look and feel of the RA structure, the style is quite different because of the radically different research process with children taking on a serious scientific identity.

Counterexamples such as the Blackawton Bees paper make the point that it is not the archive itself that is blind. The problem is the fit between the histories, technologies, knowledges, styles and institutional gatekeeping roles that create the assemblages that enable optimal packaging in a market-oriented discourse of efficiency. There are contexts, exceptions and alternatives that need to be explored to challenge and enrich how we understand what counts as knowledge and its expression in writing. At the same time as 'the measured university' (Peseta *et al.*, 2017) seems to be gaining traction with its ranking tables, predatory journals and imposter syndromes, we are in a moment where there is a surge of alternative publishing with many excellent initiatives and examples of writing differently that explicitly challenge the god view. The publication ALT DiS (Schroeder *et al.*, 2002) broke new ground in the composition/applied language studies tradition, critiquing the stifling effects of the dominant discourses in the US academy. There is also creative re-thinking in the disciplines themselves. For example, Choi *et al.* (2020) 'Critical methods for the study of world politics: Creativity and transformation' has vivid examples of writing differently. The Interventions Series in which this book is published is rich with cutting-edge, interdisciplinary titles right in the heart of Routledge, a mainstream publisher. There are other examples too such as the Slow Scholarship movement that takes its place in a long line of critiques of how knowledge-making has become a commodity.[2]

Initiatives such as these encourage us teachers of academic writing to use the archive differently and not to repeat it in its most blunt form as we reproduce only the god view in our teaching. The version/vision of scientific communication as 'faceless and passionless by design' espoused by the physics teacher quoted earlier is not the only possibility. Aspirant writers should be able to play with and explore the relationship between subjective and objective, between process and product, between trace and formal archives. Teachers of research writing need to be less transfixed by the pressures of the supermarket and more open to the practices and pedagogies of how knowledge from 'right where you are' meets the god view.

The next reflection is a reminder of Anglonormativity (McKinney, 2017) in knowledge-making processes and how we might use the archive differently. It is not just English but the scientific register with which it is compounded that can frustrate research students. A student registered for a master's degree in the Health Sciences brought her struggle to the circle:

Reflection 9
Bella comes late, flustered, rushing from a supervision session which was all about finding the right term so she can complete her proposal. She needs a concept to hold her study about becoming a mother again in another country. She's not happy with the medical term suggested, but is running out of time. She knows exactly what she wants to do in her research project, as a midwife who has been through the experience of having a second baby in another country. But there isn't a name for this experience. We play and experiment with words and come up with acronyms.

I can't remember how this resolved but I do remember her frustration and resistance to the scientific medical term. It must have been a *something*-multigravid - far too clumsy to say 'becoming a mother again in a different country' in the rich language of experience. I remember her being asked if there was a word in a southern African indigenous language that would give the experience more dignity.

Bella might have enjoyed reading Somikazi Deyi's (2014) chapter, 'A Lovely Imposition: The Complexity of Writing a Thesis in isiXhosa'. Using the format of an interview as a platform for the chapter, Somi expands the archive as she reflects on her experience of writing her master's thesis on mathematics education in isiXhosa, one of the country's official, but marginalised, languages. She describes the risks she took in confronting the contradictions in multilingual policy and practice in post-colonial settings. In spite of the difficulties with supervision and examination in isiXhosa, she embraces the chance to use her 'rich and creamy' primary language as a language of scientific expression.

I have become more aware of the limited way in which I use the archive in the scholarship I read in my own field. Even as I espouse the importance of the 'bumpy read' (Turner, 2018), it has taken me a different kind of labour and appreciation to engage with research outside of my comfort zone. I have had to learn how to use and assess translation software in order to read Academic Literacies texts in Spanish (Lillis, 2017) and can only read local publications in English. Reading Achille Mbembe's *On the Postcolony* (2001), Raewyn Connell's *Southern Theory* (2007), Jean Comaroff and John Comaroff's (2012) *Theory from the South* has opened up paths to understanding how the fallout from colonialism reinscribes inequality in domains of knowledge.

Peripheral Vision and Webbed Accounts

In thinking about the knowledge questions asked in the circle as post-graduates weigh up frameworks and styles, and in light of occlusions in my own reading, I reflect here briefly on work from three writers who have in different ways written from the margins of mainstream scholarship. All critique the way that much of mainstream scholarship coalesces around an omniscient stance that enables a vantage point of expanded neutrality. Donna Haraway's work, particularly her 1988 text, 'The Science Question in Feminism and the Privilege of Partial Perspective', is striking in that it is written from the standpoint of a life scientist who is also a feminist, or the other way round, as posed in the title. Her critique centres on the notion of what she calls the god trick which perpetuates the myth that a zero-point position is possible or desirable – that everything can be seen from a position that does not need to reveal its location. Crucially she does not distance herself from the goal of reaching for objectivity, instead coupling ideas of objective and subjective in the compound of 'embodied objectivity' in order to achieve faithful accounts of a real world that can be shared. For Haraway objectivity is not seen as above and beyond but as deeply committed to the situatedness of knowledge as an ethical project that takes responsibility for self-other relationships in knowledge-making. 'Situated knowledge' (another compound made up of what seem at first glance to be opposites) is profoundly different from the god trick which perpetuates the lie of 'seeing everything from nowhere' (1988: 581) but acknowledges that objectivity can only come with partial perspective so that we take on the ethical project of being 'answerable for what we learn to see' (and write about) in a way that does not split subjective from objective (1988: 583). This requires a commitment to 'the science and politics of interpretation, translation, stuttering, and the partially understood' (1988: 589). The ethics and politics of location needs a vulnerability to function meaningfully. Situated knowledges as a project is constantly on the move in that 'the way to find a larger vision is to be somewhere in particular' (1988: 590), an insight that Haraway says came to her while walking her dog. This kind of feminist objectivity can be taken forward by shapeshifters such as the trickster as we 'give up mastery but keep searching for fidelity, knowing that we will be hoodwinked' (1988: 593–594).

For my commitments to interweave the trace and the formal archives, it is important to me that Haraway (1988: 584) is not romantic about what it takes to work with knowledge from below:

> The standpoints of the subjugated are not 'innocent' positions [...] for *how* to see from below is a problem requiring at least as much skill and bodies and language, with the mediations of vision, as the 'highest' technoscientific visualizations.

The work of translation and partial understanding requires a form of engagement that is perhaps better understood now than it was when she wrote this paper. As a leader in Feminist New Materialist thinking and scholarship, questions of form, language and representation are taken seriously. There are journals devoted to alternative styles and politics, inviting blog entries and think pieces and publishers who are willing to take risks.[3] Moving between the god view and writing from where you are is not easy: students in the circle struggle with it; I have struggled with it in the writing of this book, in having to be specific about difficult things, in having to work with my positionality without over-simplifying or distorting. We have seen Bella's struggle with finding a word to describe the birth experience she had been through. And politics from below can also be reductionist and totalising.

The need to locate ourselves somewhere is at once physical/political – in the world – and also theoretical, since theory always comes out of specific knowledge-making contexts. We do have to take a position, but not to stake it out unshakeably with fixed vision. It can be a position that straddles, that is a shapeshifter, contingent, disruptive and openly partial, requiring ethical awareness and decision-making. In this spirit, Haraway proposes 'webbed accounts' with their tensions and charged resonances rather than 'master theory' that attempts to explain everything (1988: 588).

From a decolonial perspective, a tradition that has entered the South African academy since the #MustFall movements, Maldonado-Torres (2007) 'On the Coloniality of Being' stands out. The article is interesting for being a webbed account of the emergence of thinking about how the aftermath of colonialism shapes everyday experience. It is a vivid expression of the flux of theory in action, via theorists as diverse as Heidegger, Levinas, Dussel, Fanon, all who were interested in ontologies, though with different outworkings. Together they reveal a moving and subtle overlapping account of the conversations that shaped his thinking as part of the Modernity/Coloniality circle of South American critical theorists. Like others who critique the god view, he borrows a metaphor to do with totalising vision from Castro-Gomez (2021) – the notion of the hubris of the zero-point. Maldonado-Torres uses this notion to convey the arrogance of the assumption that knowledge is transparent and universal, and this is what makes it useful regardless of space, history, identity, making the argument that coloniality is the dark side of modernity.

Other voices who exemplify the ability to work with webbed accounts to powerful effect are bell hooks in the way she starts 'Theory as liberatory practice' (1991): 'Let me begin by saying that I came to theory because I was hurting'.[4] Imagine Ngugi wa Thiongo's *Decolonising the Mind* (1986) without his personal accounts of colonial schooling. These scholars work with embodied objectivity as partial knowledge, with the potential to re-size the Anglosphere and what it can say about knowledge and/ of the other – the intersections between colonialism and the invention of race and the need to subjugate or rescue an abject Other. They are like Haraway's tricksters, straddlers, creolised, impossible to belong to one space, even if they commit themselves to these spaces as activists.

The points of the compass – North, South, East and West – are epistemological constructions (Collyer & Dufoix, 2022). They tell us about epistemic injustice rather than territorial and geographical realities, since these cartographic representations are misleading: in the Mercator projection, the West and the North are enlarged and in the centre, while South and East are peripheral and shrivelled in size. So if a counter to the god view is what I think of as the street view – a view from below that emerges from a struggle to be heard, and to frame knowledge differently – then clearly the street view emerges everywhere, including in the Centre, or the centres in the periphery, in places like the university where I have worked. The street view can be seen in the alternative newspaper Vernac News group launched by students in the Western Cape as a challenge to the dominant Anglocentric ideologies of communication on campuses. Lwazi Mkula's (2018) thesis 'Language Ideologies and Decoloniality in Vernac

News' tells the story (http://hdl.handle.net/11427/29426). Scholarship in Southern sociolinguistics and applied linguistics (McKinney, 2017; Pennycook & Makoni, 2020; Rudwick & Makoni, 2021) is working to re-frame the way language and multilingualism are understood and how they are involved in the production of racial othering.

A connection between the dominant discourse and writing is made in Kate Cadman's concept of divine discourse. Cadman (2003) writes as an applied linguist and ex English teacher who saw the epistemic violence of her practice after having embraced feminist, Indigenous Australian and periphery scholarship. Speaking from inside the research writing pedagogy community, she asks that we find ways to interrogate the taken-for-granted assumptions that underlie postgraduate writing pedagogy and practice. These include the constraints on what counts as a relevant area of study, the criteria for assessing a thesis or journal article, the available styles that are embedded in an intellectual worldview that 'does not recognise, and therefore cannot know, the limitations of its own taken for granted, almost sacred, understandings, of what constitutes "knowledge" and its expression in the English language' (Cadman, 2003: 1).

In her chapter on a southern research writing pedagogy, Cadman (2014) explores how the traditional categories of the RA structure can be challenged and filled out in ways that invite previously subjugated knowledges. In arguing for a southern mode of knowing it becomes possible to imagine new logics for the old genre moves. For example, introduction/background sections 'might bring contexts and communities to life in ways traditionally seen as irrelevant'; and the logic of data discussion could emerge from subjective criteria such as emotional valency or communal criteria rather than thematic categories from the frameworks of metropolitan theory. Writing teachers have to learn to read for the extra-academic contexts that have given rise to the research (2013: 188–190). Embedded in these contexts will be other nascent archives that tug on orality, spirituality, forms of resistance, justice, healing and environmental practices that will require writers to swerve, traverse, strategise about what to hide and what to reveal. In short, this is a kind of writing where subjectivities will be at risk (Gibbs, 2015).

Where I take issue with Cadman is that she does not advocate transgressive practices for novice researchers as 'the conditions are not yet in place which would allow this to be viewed positively' (2014: 173). These changes will only take root when new scholars take this on in numbers rather than waiting for Anglocentric privilege to see the consequences of its blind spots. North-south, 'fresh' and 'vintage'[5] collaborations are already part of a strategic third space (Homi Bhabha, 1994) that welcomes hybridity and new forms of argumentation often made possible by innovative post-positivist methodologies as seen in the terms postcolonial, post-human and post-qualitative.

Theory as a Verb

The voices in the section above illustrate a different way of doing theory that is alive and on the move, with peripheral vision alert to what is at stake in multiple settings, a kind of stitching at the interface between god- and street views. The previous section ended with Cadman's challenge to divine discourse, which focuses on what texts might actually look like if made differently. This section explores how the god view is sustained by a cluster of discursive moves to achieve a grammar of objectivity. These centre around nominalisation – the grammatical process of turning verbal processes into nouns (as in the way the phrase 'they argued about' becomes 'the argument'), the privileging of the passive over the active voice, and deletion of personal agency. I make a case for thinking of theory as a doing – a verb rather than a noun. The search for a balance between subjective and objective in writing is a constant theme in the circle, as is clear in the stories and notes, but it is perhaps most visible when students are giving each other written feedback on their two pages.[6] Feedback was sometimes harsh, as in the online circle that went wrong when there was no facilitator as described in Chapter 1. Orthodoxies and insecurities about the shoulds of divine discourse were often expressed.

Nominalisation is a powerful platform for knowledge-building. It compacts verbal processes into nouns or noun phrases that can then become the subject of the sentence. Many argue that being able to manage these linguistic translations from concrete accounts of what happened in the flow of the moment to abstract generalisations is crucial to becoming competent in academic writing, being able to draw cause and effect connections etc. Divine discourse is not possible without a great deal of nominalisation. But there is a down-side. In a sentence like this: *'Globalization has led to increased and improved international communication'*[7] the noun globalisation becomes a congealed 'thing' – a concept to classify and generalise with. It seems to involve a stilling of the action, making the complex process seem timeless. By compacting and reifying the potentials of a process, it is presented as a fact, making it more difficult to contest, thereby reinforcing dominant power relations. With the statement starting with the noun globalisation, it is more difficult to ask questions about who says what, where, with what consequences. The correspondence between Michael Billig and J.R. Martin is an interesting account of debates about nominalisation.[8]

Nominalisation is a story with nouns and I am drawn to those that favour the story with verbs. I am not arguing against nominalisation or against objectivity, but that we remind ourselves that we have a choice, that we invite the choice, that we think about what versions of knowledge we are bringing about. Learning to speak and write like a book comes at a cost (Bangeni & Kapp, 2005).

It is possible to use grammatical metaphor the other way round, to turn nouns into verbs. The Southern inflection to the study of language and sociolinguistics mentioned earlier is accompanied by an interesting word shift that seems to underlie a broader paradigm change in the study of language. The introduction of the term *languaging* rather than 'language' is a break from monolingual ideologies that reify named languages as if they were homogenous entities waiting to be occupied by hungry consumers.[9] Turning the noun language into a verbal process of languaging is an example of grammatical metaphor done here to coin a new word that expresses the doingness rather than the thingness of language.

What if we played with the word theory in the same way that sociolinguists do with the term languaging? Changing theory to theorising doesn't quite do it. Grappling with the difference between our lived professional worlds and how we wrote about them, and with the way we induct postgraduate students into theoretical camps, fellow literacies traveller Lynn Coleman and I have discussed these difficulties in what we called our café conversations where we met off campus. These meetings were not unlike the circle in that we can try out ideas before taking them upstream. We have written a paper about this (Coleman & Thesen, 2018) where we take our scholarly identities with us into the café space but turn them into rougher street view conversations. Over time, and through our difficult conversations and the dilemmas they raise, we started to ask what theory does in helping us approach the complex issues that face us in our work in academic literacies. Theoretical work is not regarded as a strength in our field of education development, a hybrid relatively new sub-specialisation in the field of higher education where our work in Academic Literacies is nested.

Working and writing together, we began to think of theory as a verb, drawing on Brian Street's (1993) notion of culture as a verb. For Street, the question is not what *is* culture, but what does it *do*. Like essentialist definitions of culture, theory can divide and school-build as much as it explains. One of the invisible aspects of theory building is the semiotic activity that underlies it. I have already touched on nominalisation as foundational in academic discourse. All academics and academics-in-the-making encounter theory through reading – mainly through journal articles, which are typically expressed through text that has to be in the right place in the RA model introduced earlier. In the fields that I work in and arguably for much of the humanities and social sciences, the default is to identify a problem, ask a question, choose a theory and commit to it, and then straighten the line so your findings can be read through the classificatory lens of this theory. If one straightens the line from taking a theoretical position, committing to a framework and a position, one has to be true to this theoretical stance in the construction of the final product, to tell a coherent story. The story is filled out with the help of its methodology, together the two select what it is possible to see and to say. There is little room for anything outside of this. To stretch a point, the grammar of the research article resembles subject-verb-object: the subject is theory, the verb is methodology, and the object is some chosen aspect of higher education – often the student. The research process on the other hand is an immersive process of discovery, a story with verbs. But the conversion of the process into a product involves a translation into the conventions of the genres for journal articles. No wonder we recycle deficit notions of the student: with students always in the object position, they are pinned down and held back, as we attempt to honour the integrity of the theory, rather than the lived lives – contradictions, dilemmas, false starts and all – of the people in these spaces.

We are looking for another way to do theory, to take it out of its rei-fied, school-building boxes, to make it more processual, relational and convivial. Rather than fixing, strengthening or codifying theory so that it sits as a solid, reified thing – theory as a noun – we think of it as a verb; a process, responsive, in flux and in the life of individuals as they make sense over time. The project of classifying theories and genres is not the only way, or even a particularly productive way, to proceed; it is not equal to the complexity of these times.

Surface Tension

As an act of using theory as a verb, this chapter ends in an exploration of surface tension as a form of inventive interference in the workings of the god view. The idea first came to me while watching insects on a pond – the pond suggestive of the support offered by the circle while students were on a journey elsewhere. I take the concept of surface tension out of its relatively settled home in the physical sciences and into the writers' circle and outwards into the teaching of research writing. It is an attempted translation across domains that stutters and hesitates since I can't access it from the specialist language of science. I hope to use it in the spirit that engages the critical questions posed by Law and Urry (2004: 397) and taken up by Coleman and Ringrose (2013): 'is it possible to imagine developing methods that strengthen particular realities while eroding others?'. More specifically, how might surface tension be used to illuminate the potentials of the writers' circle as a problem space for thinking about the relationship between writing and knowledge-making? Can it be used to illuminate interfaces without annihilating either side?

In introducing Deleuze and Guattari's *A Thousand Plateaus* (1987), Massumi writes that in the spirit of rhizomatic thought, 'A concept is a brick'. It is doing something, either building or destroying, and in trying to make sense of its workings, we can only say, 'it depends'. More must be known about the circumstances. The brick is circumstances-in-action, a vector, an act at a volatile juncture (1987: xii–xiii). In this book, the concept of surface tension is the brick. There is no easy translation of it, no neat correspondence between language and what it represents. The rhizomatic concept is a verb. It is in motion between subject and object, interfering with the story with nouns. It needs collaborative, vulnerable-making work to be interpreted in context. If we use the potentials of grammatical metaphor to turn the adjective (noun?) 'surface' in surface tension into a verb, my project is to surface the tensions and alienation that many postgraduate writers find themselves living with. The tensions are between what is inside and what is outside – between the felt experience of trying to write your way into a research focus while the discourses and language available are constraining and alienating. In this sense, it is possible to bring surface tension to think about the body, and to its surface (skin) as profoundly relational: the interface where inside (feeling, affect, subjectivity) meets outside (social structures, the gaze). This idea is picked up again in Chapter 5 when I explore time and the 'itch' to write, in Reflection 11 on page 85.

In the formal archive, surface tension is owned by the physical sciences and the STEM disciplines where it refers to a subtle yet extremely powerful phenomenon of contact which comes into play when phases – gas, liquid, solid – come into contact, most notably for us when a liquid is in contact with air. When dew drops form in a nasturtium leaf, different substances have come together, making something new take place. What makes the drop cling and hold its form is the interplay of different forces leading to the tightening of molecules on the surface of the water, enabling it to retain its shape, at least for a while. In a body of water, molecules attract one another equally as cohesive forces to enable the water to retain its character. But when water molecules encounter air, or the surface of a leaf, the bonds are broken. There is a different force operating at the surface: here molecules have fewer of their own kind to bond with, so they join together to resist the air they're in contact with. This creates an elasticity which reduces the surface area and enables new possibilities. This elasticity enables a bubble to hold its shape, or a dewdrop to form a perfect sphere or a drop of mercury to refuse to scatter. It also enables a paperclip – made from metal or plastic with greater density than water – to be held on the surface, appearing to float.

This image of paperclips floating in a small pond shows this phenomenon (see Figure 3.1). Interesting things are happening at the edges, where the clip is in touch with the water, and where the water is in contact with the stone bowl.

This small bit of theatre staged as an experiment (or experiment staged as theatre?) helped me to think about the circle and try out the idea of surface tension, holding one moment in an open-ended journey of discovery. This functioned as a thought experiment when I was primarily interested in the cohesion in the circle, thinking about the circle as a safe space, as explored in Chapter 1. The thought process went something like this: the stone bowl and the cluster of water-worn pebbles are there anyway, in a suburban courtyard. Sometimes there is water in the font-like

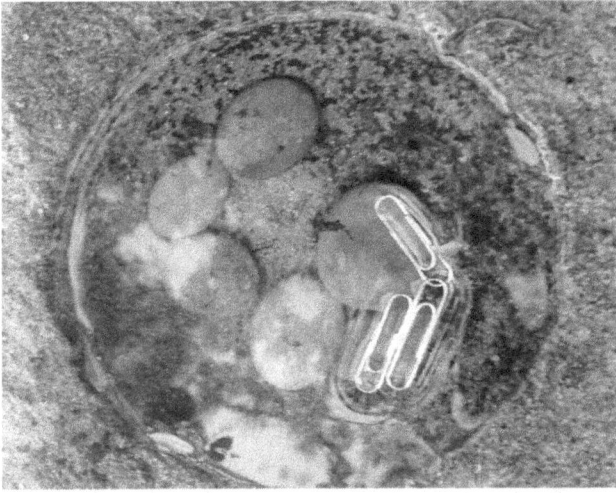

Figure 3.1 Surface tension as paper clips are held on the surface of water

bowl. Sometimes, when the bowl is full, the contact between the water and stone bowl is distinct, a bulge at the edge. Tiny leaves from a jacaranda tree fall into the water, gravitating to the edge. Surface tension enters my thought flow – a memory retrieved from a science class in high school – along with words like sink and float, cling. The bowl and the pebbles suggest the writers' circle. The paperclips are artifice, an idea from a Google search where the phenomenon of surface tension is often illustrated by experiments with paper clips. As useful objects they also suggest attempts to organise the two pages of writing that are the currency in the circle, to find a place for them in the archive.

Returning to the scene pictured above, with water brimming and the paper clips afloat in the pond: a day later, the situation has changed. Wind and sun have caused the water to evaporate, leaving the leaves stranded on the cement edge, now dry. A rain squall could also have broken the elasticity on the surface, and the paperclips are now on the bottom, resting on the stones.

Extending the translation further beyond the courtyard experiment with a stone bowl and paperclips, there are generative ways to use the concept. One of the epigraphs at the beginning of this chapter is a small moment in Rachel Cusk's (2014) novel where surface tension is taken from her book to a different place, to front this chapter. Her writing itself gives shape to the surface tension at the interface between the interior of the researcher/writer's experience, how it is lived and held on to, and the exterior – the audience, readership. The tension of the surface is never resolved, always productive. The two pages that writers bring to the circle are a portal between two worlds, interior and exterior, between air and water, between the messy, exploratory world of living as a postgraduate, in which uncertainty and self-doubt are strongly felt, and the often daunting, emotionally austere practice of making new knowledge, in writing, in English. Forces that work in different directions (both supporting and unifying and dispersing and multiplying) are temporarily held in balance, in dynamic equilibrium, in relation to one another.

But surface tension is not always supporting and positive which is how I thought of it initially with the notion of safe space. It seemed to be associated with floating and buoyancy as I searched for an affirming way to describe the circle. But if you are a body in movement through or on water, a swimmer or in a boat, it is the quality of the interface that establishes the friction that holds you back. While on the one hand it enables a vessel to float, on the other it creates drag or friction that interferes with movement.

What is so generative about the idea for me is that it is at its core relational – the 'something more' that comes about when surfaces are in contact. Surface tension is more than the sum of its parts. A key affordance of surface tension is elasticity – the property of holding while stretching. This is where the trace lives. It is also porous, asking questions at the interface, surfacing the tensions if thought of as a verb, a doing, revealing not dichotomies but both/ands – a space of entanglement where there are only openings and ways through, though these might be in unexpected directions. This elasticity in the circle is evident in the opening stories in this chapter, where I recall how students explored the edge of the discourses of their disciplines: Ellen found a new hybrid concept for her research while both Elizabeth and Bella explored uptake for their desire to innovate – Elizabeth to use an image on the first page of her thesis and Bella to find a new term that did not betray something that mattered deeply.

As a concept-in-action, surface tension both unsettles and stabilises this inquiry into the interface between trace and formal archive. I have arrived at this point through different forms of interference most of which don't appear on the surface of the final text at all. It feels as if these are integral to the product even if some of them are only briefly described rather than realised. These processes are all unsettling in some way, creating dilemmas of reflexivity and othering, allowing in the unexpected, or slowing me down in some way, like the swimmer where the fictional drag at the surface is the problem to be solved. This interference has to include the ethical relational work of acknowledging my positionality in the project of running the circle and also of writing this book. This work is also part of the surface tension.

In the next chapter we go back to the circle but not via written text as traditionally understood. Particularly in the early days of the circle, the circle announced itself through laughter. But how to explore this form of communication, which is almost impossible to represent in language? How to work the seam between writing and laughing? The next chapter explores what animates laughter in the circle, at the interface between archives.

Notes

(1) Charles Darwin's *Origin of the Species*, first published in 1859, provides a fascinating counterexample. In what looks like an early version of referencing, Darwin writes that he has been '…most kindly favoured with skins from several quarters of the world including the Hon. W. Elliot from India…' and goes on to observe that 'The diversity of the breeds is something astonishing. Compare the English carrier and the short-faced tumbler and see the wonderful difference in their beaks…' (2009: 20–21). When I ask students in writing workshops 'Is this scientific?', they typically say no, the author uses I, there are no references, you can't use adjectives like 'remarkable'. The obsession with objectivity is a modern invention with the growth of scientific institutions.

(2) The LSE Impact blog https://blogs.lse.ac.uk/impactofsocialsciences/ is a rich source of discussion on these issues. See for example Filip Vostal https://blogs.lse.ac.uk/impactof-socialsciences/2021/05/11/four-reasons-slow-scholarship-will-not-change-academia/

(3) There are some powerful examples in our book on risk in academic writing (Thesen & Cooper, 2014). Suresh Canagarajah and Ena Lee's (2014) extended account of a failed journal publishing collaboration, Moeain Arend's (2014) 'It was hardly about writing' brings Actor Network Theory to light as the contributors innovate with form as they bring the trace archive to their writing. Somi Deyi's (2014) chapter mentioned earlier is another example, as it uses the interview as a dialogic way of exploring the trace.

(4) The rest of the opening goes like this: 'The pain within me was so intense that I could not go on living. I came to theory desperate, wanting to comprehend - to grasp what was happening around and within me. Most importantly, I wanted to make the hurt go away. I saw in theory then a location for healing. I came to theory young, when I was still a child. In *The Significance of Theory* (1990: 1) Terry Eagleton says: 'Children make the best theorists, since they have not yet been educated into accepting our routine social practices as "natural", and so insist on posing to those practices the most embarrassingly general and fundamental questions, regarding them with a wondering estrangement which we adults have long forgotten. Since they do not yet grasp our social practices as inevitable, they do not see why we might not do things differently'.

(5) The categories 'fresh' and 'vintage' were introduced in our Writing Centre at UCT to distinguish between old hands and new voices among the postgraduate students employed as writing tutors each year.

(6) A reminder that these written responses on two pages are not part of my record of the circle in the yellow folders, as students took these hand-written comments home with them.

(7) This example is discussed in Liardet (2015).

(8) There is a lively debate about nominalisation and the way linguists write in *Discourse & Society*. Michael Billig (2008) critiques the way discourse analysts, particularly Systemic Functional Linguists, write, arguing that they are blind to the effects of their own analytical categories. They have turned a process into a thing. J.R. Martin (2008) presents the other pole of the debate. Billig looks into critical discourse analysis, its categories of analysis, particularly nominalisation and use of the passive, and how these translate into a writing surface that is at odds with its underlying principles.

(9) McKinney's 2017 chapter 'What Counts as [a] Language?' gives a clear account of challenges to monolingual Anglonormative ideologies.

4 HA HA HA: Shaking the Tree of Language

'[Laughter] has a knack of baffling every effort, of slipping away and escaping, only to bob up again, a pert challenge flung at philosophical speculation'.

Henri Bergson (1914: 1)
Laughter: An Essay on the Meaning of the Comic

Colleagues and students in our building often commented on the laughter that they heard spilling out of the room where the circle met regularly. Laughter is the quintessential sign of the trace as it deflates orthodoxy and august images of the postgraduate scholar while it also creates solidarity. But it is difficult to research as it cannot be rendered into language. I describe how I have stayed with the laughter over time, thinking with different theories in an open-ended way. Affective methodologies help to reflect on what laughter does and means in the lives of students in the circle, as I explore connections to affect more widely. The chapter includes an account of a workshop to reflect on laughter in the circle.

Staying with the Laughter

When our team started offering writers' circles through the Writing Centre, the concept of the writing group was a novelty. In the early days of trying to understand our practice, aware that we were trying to do something different, we recorded a discussion with Clement who was leading the circle at the time, asking him about the ingredients for a successful circle. He surprised us, saying 'If they're not laughing, watch out!'. Laughter seemed to be a sign of vitality and renewal, a joyful expression of life, and also a provocation: writing pedagogy was no longer shrouded in silence (Starke-Meyerring, 2014: 65). It seemed to provoke the studious space around it, to dare the university to take itself less seriously. Laughter in the circle was unpredictable, sometimes disconcerting, and through the years it has felt worth staying with as it seems to gesture to where the trace lives. The phrase 'staying with' echoes Donna Haraway's *Staying with the Trouble* (2016) as a political commitment not to run away from the meshing and complexity, to work, play and think in a space of ambiguity that does justice to the density of contemporary knowledge-making.

But researching laughter presents challenges. It is an outworking of affect that is almost impossible to research as it clings to the edge of language. For the language and literacy teacher-researcher, laughter defies any easy mapping of sign and signifier since it cannot be easily expressed in language. It is also difficult to interpret as it takes us in to the domain of affect in such a visceral, embodied way. Massumi (2015: viii) writes that to '"think through" affect is to continue its life-filling, life-forming journey'. In trying to stay with affect we get some insight into being 'right where you are' (2015: xi), airing a kind of 'wiggle room' (2015: 6) that reminds us that a next step is possible, even as a mode of resistance to power relations that coagulate around writing as a form of capital. This chapter stays with the laughter in various forms of enquiry over time. Part of the method here is to interact with theory in a more organic way, getting close to how we encounter it in the process of thinking. I bring theorising in as a resource for sense-making over time and narrate something of that journey. This is done in combination with different registers and modes to de-centre the god view so that new configurations and possibilities may flourish.

In an early attempt to stay with the laughter, I wrote about moments in the circle where laughter surfaced (Thesen, 2014). One moment centred on a discussion of procrastination after I had shared an extract from Geoff Dyer's account of trying to write the biography *Out of Sheer Rage: Wrestling with DH Lawrence* (1998). We discussed how this extract resonated with our experience as writers. Nell spoke about how in working with literatures, she prolonged the reading and delayed the writing: 'I think you need to have a crush on your theorist, enough of a crush to keep you going through the thesis', she advised. As we laughed about the seduction of theory, theorists' looks, politics, foibles, the difference between flirting (on the internet) and having a crush on a theorist, the laughter in the circle seemed to play with and deflate the image of the researcher as disembodied, cerebral, white and male, to bend the image of the researcher, and of theory itself, to a different image – intense, personal and consequential.

There was a sombre side – an underbelly of struggle – that accompanied these moments that I recalled. In one circle, Clement asked participants to draw how they felt at that point in their research. This 'transmodal moment' from languaging to drawing enables a shift in orientation (Newfield, 2014: 6). Figure 4.1 shows how Ellen expressed her feeling of being stuck.

Her sketch shows a desk with papers piled high, books stacked on the right and printouts of drafts spilling over on the left. In the centre is a small, terrified pop-eyed cartoon face peering over the back of a chair at an animated open laptop, with sharp teeth defining its edges. An electrical

Figure 4.1 Ellen's sketch of stuckness

cord, drawn with a heavy hand and darker line, seems to have a life of its own as it rears up from the plug in the wall, from which it has come adrift. The sketch is a form of trace-work that illuminates the surface tension in research writing, suggesting how the trace and formal archives may co-exist. We laugh, but Ellen asks: 'We're having fun and laughing, but this makes me depressed. Are we actually enjoying this stuckness?'. Laughing seems to lead quickly to more uncomfortable feelings. Our shared laughter seems to accentuate our feelings of shame when we are unable to make progress.

Another moment of laughter that I recall is in the particularly challenging circle described in some detail in Chapter 1. The circle had been shot through with tensions. As facilitator, it was difficult to give shape to a circle that was going wrong as Jo struggled to write about her research participants without giving offence. Elizabeth came to the rescue, miming our different reactions: 'disbelief, sorrow, relief, scepticism, and scholarly concern in turn. Laughter unites us' (see page 23). Laughter rescued us and enabled us to move on.

In a transmodal exploration in the circle some years later, in a quick warm-up activity before we reviewed the two pages for the day, I invited participants to draw a concept they were busy writing about. I did not collect these as data as I was trying to steer away from being too forensic about the circle. I also took part in the activity and chose laughter as my concept. The drawing is shown in Figure 4.2.

I used orange and purple crayons. The profile is distorted, with fat cheeks, a dimple, exaggerated mouth and nostril, eyes screwed up. There is a puff of breath, then the wordsounds, HA HA HA, which seem to override the tentative words *writ...ting* and *laughter* – and beyond the wordsounds there are some impersonal figures in the shape of cut-out dolls. The words (are they words?) ha ha ha are wholly inadequate, and like the static row of cut-out dolls, are not up to the task of expressing the full-bodied complexity of the laughing person. In the drawing, the mouth is not at the centre of the composition. It is off centre, against the right-hand edge of the page. For some reason that is lost to me, I drew the face off-centre. Perhaps the gap on the left leaves space for an unexpressed other, a relational co-laugher, or an object of laughter. A portrait of one person laughing does not make sense, particularly if the portrait is in profile. We are always laughing *at* or *with* someone or something.

Figure 4.3 echoes medical drawings of the cortical homunculus with the distorted profile of the face. Perhaps I made an unconscious connection to images like this. In an attempt to be true to two kinds of representational logic, one verbal, the other visual, these scientific drawings create a bizarre mapping of the cortex, showing the intensity of neural pathways. The mouth, with lips, teeth, tongue, is always disproportionately large, because of the sheer neural traffic that pulses through them. The hands, particularly the thumb, are also distorted.

Figure 4.2 Drawing laughter as a concept

In the medical drawing, parts of the cortex are mapped to bodily functions. The labelling is on the inside of the drawing. In the extract selected from the diagram, language is on the left. We have a set of labels that denotes objectively identifiable parts of the body and superordinate functions (mastication, vocalisation) but the visual on the right is distorted. The mouth, nostrils are out of proportion, and way too big. Classification trumps the accurate denotational relationships between parts and whole. Drawings such as this may have informed the hand-drawn concept that I created in the circle.

The process of drawing has shaken the tree of language, displacing language, reducing it in the drawing to the word-sounds HA HA HA, and drawing attention to the necessary impossibility/fallacy that we can accurately represent laughter, or any other aspect of life on the move, though it is important to try. Instead of seeking representational accuracy, this chapter chooses a rhizomatic, zig-zagging sideways approach. Deleuze and Guattari (1987: 7-8) put it well in this argument for a method that decentres language:

> It is always possible to break a language down into internal structural elements, an undertaking not fundamentally different from a search for roots. There is always something genealogical about a tree. It is not a method for the people. A method of the rhizome type, on the contrary, can analyze language only by decentering it into other dimensions and other registers.

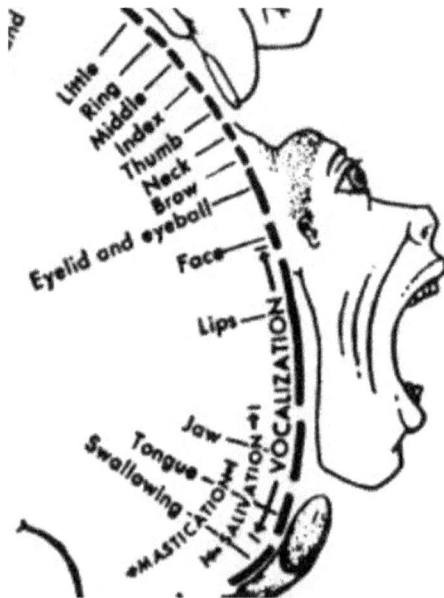

Figure 4.3 Cortical homunculus[1]

The stories and drawings springing from my engagement with the circle have tried this decentring into other dimensions and registers. They now give way to engaging with other writers who have been intrigued by laughter as a social phenomenon.

Staying in Touch

Laughter scatters and gathers and flows. Thinking with laughter is not amenable to the conventional structure of the research piece within divine discourse, which asks us to commit to a theory and work consistently with it through to the conclusion. I try to do something different here in the form of a narrative about some of the interpretive work that I have engaged with over time. This is what Karen Barad (2012: 207) calls being in touch: 'What keeps theories alive and lively is being responsible and responsive to the world's patternings and murmurings'. I tried early on in this exploration over time to theorise laughter, drawing particularly on Bakhtin (1968), who was familiar to me as a philosopher of language. His work on the carnival element as renewal and upending spoke to my interest in laughter in the circle. Laughter is always ambivalent, 'it asserts and denies; it buries and revives' (1968: 12). It can:

> [...] consecrate inventive freedom, to permit the combination of a variety of elements and their rapprochement, to liberate from the prevailing point of view of the world, from conventions and established truths, from cliché [it] offers the chance to have a new outlook on the world. (1968: 34)

The power of Bakhtin is that he takes an historical angle on laughter, showing how it went underground in the Enlightenment, squashed out sideways to express itself in a range of other ways ever since. There is no room for laughter in the god view. It is suppressed with the emphasis on rationality and objectivity detached from the body, in search of a universal position outside the messiness, contradictions and desires of the everyday.

In previous writing on laughter (Thesen, 2014: 172) I argued that 'laughter is a sign of life' and quoted Bakhtin's reference to Aristotle's 'of all living creatures only man is endowed with laughter' (in Bakhtin, 1968: 68). Since engaging with the notion of materiality and Deleuzian flattened ontology, I have become more interested in how the human is displaced from the centre. Cynthia Willett asks the question, 'Can the animal subaltern laugh?' (2014: 29–59), as she prizes open an interesting line of thought about interspecies ethics, at the same time enabling us to tackle oppressive norms about what is masked by not thinking beyond the frame of the human.

Reading Michael Billig's (2005) social critique of humour, I see that I have been trapped in what he calls 'ideological positivism' (2005: 5) about laughter: a sentimentality about laughter as a good thing – an expression of community in the circle. He traces a compelling web of humour, and its shadow side – ridicule – and the dual functions of laughter, to both discipline and rebel (2005: 202 ff). It is not a unitary concept, best understood as embedded in a series of paradoxes: it is both universal *and* particular, social *and* anti-social, mysterious, resistant to analysis, *and* at the same time, understandable and analysable.

This resonates with the idea that laughter comes from incongruity (Bergson, 1914) to emerge in the gap between the concreteness of bodies and language and its infinite play when things 'go wrong'. In this sense laughter is a-representational because it alerts us to where things have become 'crusted'. Emily Herrings's (2020) short piece on laughter argues that '[...]laughter solves a serious human conundrum: how to keep our minds and social lives elastic'. This elasticity, like surface tension, is a phenomenon of contact, more than the sum of its parts, where affect will be strongly felt and lived.

Helen Verran's (1999) interest in staying with the laughter in her role as a lecturer, responsible for supporting students as they learnt to teach mathematics and science in postcolonial classrooms, is sustained over time. The unorthodox, creative solutions used by a bilingual teacher as he blended English and Yoruba, each having a different concept of number, led to the sort of laughter from the savvy children, and from her, 'that grows from seeing a certainty disrupted to become a different sort of certainty: a certainty that sees itself' (1999: 138). The laughter she describes seems to live at the interface between ways of knowing, a sort of metacommentary in the 'ontic domain' – a dynamic, emergent enactment of colliding worlds (1999: 153). Her interest in laughter in mathematics classrooms did not go away. In a later paper (2007), Verran writes of the importance of learning to generalise in developing a concept of number, but what she learnt from the children 'was that it is just as important to be able to dissolve and promiscuously (re)constitute new sorts of framings and to know that and how you are doing this' (2007: 39). If we take this to writing, it is just as important to be able to have one's work received as hoped/intended in the public domain as it is to stretch the surface in writing, to find some elasticity through re-framing, experimenting, taking risks. Perhaps tracing the laughter in the circle can help to explore this interface, where the tensions that shape the process of writing one's research play out.

This brief exploration of laughter challenged me to go further with laughter, to think about it beyond my subjectivity in the circle, where particularly in the early days of the circle, there was pressure on us to evaluate our new pedagogy and show that it was working. If we are having fun, surely that is a good thing? But it doesn't lend itself to numbers or any easy claims about 'success'. In the next section I describe how ideas from a workshop I attended on using concepts to re-search gave me a way back into thinking about laughter in the circle, by trying out a method from the workshop with a group of students from the circle. In this way I could try to hold subjectivity back in the design of an inquiry with others from the circle.

Concepts from the Thought Flow

A path for further exploration of laughter in the circle opened up at a workshop on post-qualitative inquiry.[2] We were a group of academics from across the four universities in the Western Cape region, all of us interested in doing academia differently. Coming together over several years, participation on the course gave us courage to try out new approaches to reading and writing as teachers and as researchers. I drew on my experience in the circle to inform the writing workshops that I offered on these courses, and was in turn stimulated and challenged by the ideas we explored as we sought to replenish notions of what is possible in academic discourse. In a key event, Elmarie Costandius introduced us to working with concepts. While Deleuze thought of working with concepts as the domain of philosophy, Elmarie saw working with concepts as a form of creativity, quite possible to do in a humble way with a group of educators. An art teacher steeped in Deleuzian methodologies and with a commitment to transformative practice, Elmarie guided us through a process of creating and exploring concepts in their intrinsic variability and mutation rather than their fixedness. The emphasis is not on the extent to which you can assemble a framework, and then take it, while keeping the framework intact, to social life in all its flux and confusion. It is the relations between the maker/writer/creator and the stuff that is around us that becomes important. This stuff – the thought flow, a kind of hum – is picked up on by Smith from Deleuze's lectures: 'Imagine the universal thought flow as a kind of interior monologue, the interior monologue of everyone who thinks [...] The concept is a system of singularities extracted from a thought flow' (Smith, 2012: 70). Like the notion of the concept as a brick introduced in Chapter 3, the concepts each of us worked with become a form of diffraction as 'a mapping of interferences, not of replication, reflection or reproduction (Haraway (2004: 69) in Costandius, 2019: 4).

I chose laughter as my concept, feeling challenged and keen to continue my thinking journey. Elmarie (2019: 3) guided us gently into the workshop: 'All concepts will be mapped on a big piece of paper so that new concepts can be formed by combining previous ones. In a very modest way, we will be steering away from the universal by following a simple process of linking unrelated concepts [...] we hope that these linking exercises and zigzag engagements open up new thoughts and images [...] a path set off by the spark of creation, unpredictable, undisciplined, anti-disciplinary and non-static'. We made new connections, loosely mapping concepts, stumbling on associations between disparate elements, inviting chance. Elmarie asked us to force an association between our concept and an animal or plant. I wrote down the creatures I associated with laughter: *hyena*, [praying] *mantis, venus fly trap*. MOUTH OPEN is in capital letters. These are all unusual creatures, a bit fantastical.

In travelling with the original concept of laughter, guided by Elmarie's workshop, I arrived at an altered concept, the Afrikaans word bekvol. We concluded with a spontaneously written paragraph on our new concepts, which informed this paragraph:

> Vol+bek, a full mouth. Mouth-full. Not mondvol – that would be the human mouth. Bek is an animal word. Bekvol also plays on gatvol. Fedup, with connotations from gat, meaning hole, or more graphically in Afrikaans, asshole. Laughter wants bodies. It is the thing that seizes you and rocks you and you're not always in control of it. It's the greased lightning that enables you to slip through the portal to change state. It is like the two pages, our currency in the circle. The laughter surely won't end up on the final thesis page. But it will remind us that we are social beings. It will nourish, surprise, give us a sense of presence. It propels us, keeps the momentum. It shakes us and bits fall off. Laughter interrupts language, for better or worse. You can't laugh and talk at the same time. You can't eat and laugh at the same time. You will choke, or spit it all out, and be embarrassed. Or ashamed. Shame.

Shame is an interesting word since in South African English as it is also widely used as an expression of sympathy. It suggests that shame is a deeply relational form of embodiment and that within it lie possibilities for ethical action (Probyn, 2005; Probyn *et al.*, 2019). This is a concept that introduced itself alongside laughter. A flock of concepts to do with affect. Shame and other feelings go underground and then return later in this chapter.

At the Water Point, Again

After the workshop with Elmarie, I organised a similar workshop process for circlers for us to explore laughter together. I was excited about the method used in the workshop and wanted to share it with them and to extend and deepen my inquiry into laughter. I invited a group of mainly vintage circlers to come to a workshop scheduled for a Friday afternoon rather than the usual Thursday. My email invitation was headed 'Would you like to take part in a once-off laughing (not writing) circle?'. I reminded them about the book project. 'One of the generative concepts I'd like to explore [in the book about the circle] is laughter. This is obviously a challenge. So I've come up with an idea for how to explore it together, based on a method for working with concepts that I was exposed to at a recent workshop on post-qualitative research'. The core of the group of eight that arrived was a tight cohort of PhDs who sometimes saw each other socially, most of whom had recently graduated: for them, the circle had been a crucial part of their research process, providing a space for depth of friendship, critique and ongoing solidarity. It was a reunion of sorts, an opportunity for connection and reflection. Perhaps for some there was curiosity about the research that I was doing. There is also a culture in the circle of supporting each other at events where we present our research.

While we are gathering in the meeting room, Adam comes by to say hello. The room fills. There's a lot of greeting, hugging, introductions. Elena has brought a lemon cake. She updates us on her post-PhD writing projects, while finding her body again, 'as we all do after a PhD'; Elizabeth hears that she has just missed seeing Adam – 'Adam, *ke* Adam was here and I missed him?'. She remembers him by his master's research project on the use of the discourse marker 'ke' in isiXhosa. Natasha remembers that she has forgotten an important anniversary. I'm nervous, as this isn't the usual circle. How much must I explain? My credibility as a researcher feels on the line. I have some notes, say something about Clement's observation that laughter is the key to a successful circle, mention difficulties with researching affect and a desire to avoid extractive ends-and-means relationships and forms of research. I ask if we can talk ethics at the end of the gathering. A general ethics form has already been circulated.

Then I interrupt myself as the rhythms of the usual circle meeting take over and I say, 'But let's first catch up'. Now we are coming together at the water point, again. We go around the room, briefly catching up. Then back to me, and I introduce the activity. We are going to go sideways and shake the tree of language in an exploration of laughter. We are interested in chance, play and actively forcing new connections. Some of them know about my 'obsession' with laughter as I had brought two pages of an early draft for them to comment on in the circle. I hand out the graph paper to write on.

Our concept is laughter. We go through a process where I want to get everyone to the point where they have done a freewrite to generate ideas[3] about laughter in the circle, from there we can share some keywords in the group. I adapt the steps that Elmarie took us through at the workshop. The last three steps are outlined below.

- Force a connection with a randomly assigned object handed out (a rubber egg, some chalk, pencil sharpener, a drawer from a miniature wooden cabinet on my desk, a packet of mixed spice are some objects that I recall bringing to the gathering).
- Do a freewrite for five minutes with the prompt,[4] 'When I think of laughter in the circle, ... ' – you can draw, use any language. I explain briefly about freewriting. After the freewrite, participants underline the words/phrases that stand out for them because they have some weight, are important or perhaps surprising.
- Finally, we offer the underlined words for the table. Participants don't read each other's freewrites, though I have access to them after the event.

We go through the activity. People seem to be absorbed, and at times, sceptical. I pitched them straight into this activity, without the supportive process of the workshop with Elmarie.

We use the underlined words and phrases as the basis for a conversation together and go round the circle starting with Kay. We note the differences, most strongly evident in Tia, Natasha and Vuyo's chosen words that I return to below. The sense of safe space is strong for most though. Perhaps this is because they have finished their PhDs and there is some nostalgia for the circle.

After the workshop Tia talks about the difficult moments that she recalled, not the laughter. We talk about including participation in the circle in the controversial new Memorandum of Understanding between student and supervisor and whether it is a good idea for students to mention that they attend a weekly writers' circle. More news is shared. At the end, I hand out the general ethics forms I had written for my faculty ethics committee. We talk about the ethics process for this meeting. I suggest I write the chapter up and share it with everyone.

Later I read the freewrites from the workshop, going deeper to see where the words took them, and where they take me. The freewrites offer strings of thought close to the flickering, emergent qualities of being alive, as they think through affect with the concept of laughter in the context of the circle. Freewriting is the perfect companion for the water point. Many of the words and phrases underlined (like 'gift of companionship', 'community', 'gels', 'comfortable', 'connect', 'has a loyal ring', 'kinship') endorse the sense of laughter in the circle as a communal good connected to safe space. Kay has written:

> I think of a warm glow and a place of belonging...a small and fragile cocoon of togetherness and connection. I think of the times I've cracked jokes or made smart-aleck remarks in order to cover up a sensitivity or a vulnerability or to cause a *step-change* in the tone of group if it's become overly serious or emotional.

The word 'step-change' that Kay has underlined hooks me, a reminder of how affect can shift us between states and of how laughter can assert and deny, bury and revive. Her word opens a small window in for me. It is laughter *plus* other stuff – feeling, memory, possibility. It is never on its own. There's always more. So the words that stay with me lead to what is next to, or on the other side of laughter. For Tia, the underlined words are 'I struggle', 'racist', 'horrendous', 'not something I can join in with' and 'sobering'. What is most important to her is the stuff that is 'sandwiched between laughter':

> I struggle because the most profound moments were actually not the ones where people laughed. It was where something struck me or made me rethink. My default is to not take things too seriously, to be sarcastic, [...] so for me to be jolted, to sit up and be serious is more significant. An

example is when someone explained their experience of being 'coloured' at university, an inappropriate question, a *racist* comment that makes you realise what people are researching is <u>so</u> personal. And while other people can laugh off such horrendous infringements of their rights, is to me impressive. *But not something I can join in with* [...] These times, that jolt me from my relaxed demeanour and make me think, are always sandwiched between laughter I guess.

For Vuyo, there is also a powerful slide sideways from laughter. Words such as 'connectivity' and 'beauty' are underlined in the first part of her freewrite, with a transition to 'embrace each other's [...] sores, ugliness' but later in her freewrite, 'fake' and 'potency' are underlined.

Unburdening loads, connectivity, serenity, for a moment in time equality...And it was wonderful our joy is real but at a created space which has a time duration. Oh but in that moment there is wonder, beauty, freedom, lightheartedness, scars momentarily soothed our eyes ears open to each other. We laugh and we *embrace each other's* burdens, *sores, ugliness* and we meet in a circle of humanness buoyed up by laughter. Each is aware at least I think that it is a fleeting moment....no foundation baseless but real in that we do see each other in that laughing space. It's *fake* but. and so therein lies its *potency*, better grasp it because its benefits are real there is lightheartedness afterwards for. And with that as the laughter dies down and the smiles disappear so goes the moment but yes wonderful it was to the ever so weary soul – blinded by invisibility.

What stays with me are phrases 'for a moment in time equality' and at the end, 'the ever so weary soul – blinded by invisibility'. Her thought process seems to have been cut off in 'It's *fake*.' Later while reading this chapter for ethics feedback, she explained the word fake and how once, when a circle member had not recognised her at a coffee shop, the circle had not felt like a safe space.

In Natasha's freewrite, it's her underlined word 'slog' that stands out for me, as she doesn't recall the laughter, recognising that if there had been more laughter in the circle, she might have stayed for longer. Clement was right, if they're not laughing, watch out. Her ending, which she hasn't underlined, stands out for me, 'sometimes doing academia is sore'.

When I think of laughter in the Thursday circle I think of an anomaly I don't feel like it is there I feel like there is *listening* and *compassion* & opening and things like that but also some seriousness and an edge and probably if there were more laughter & less seriousness I would have stayed for longer, enjoyed it more. But laughter is also not something one can *force* and even when I had to think of when or a space where I would laugh easily it didn't readily spring to mind. Why is that I wonder, why is it I couldn't think of space that were easy to laugh in. I thought of the *mountain* and that seemed strange but I suppose I do find that I can laugh and take myself *less seriously* [...] but I also am *too serious* I think and take things to heart too easily and you know, just need space to be able to let it go & usually the hard *slog* of an uphill on the mountain, the fresh air, the openness leads me to that release of just being able to laugh about things [...] So in the circle I don't suppose it was too easy to joke. Maybe because academics are sensitive people actually or because sometimes doing academia is sore. It hurts and so people are on the defensive.

She doesn't use the word, but it seems to be about solace, the comfort of the hard questions in the slog between the lightness of laughter and soreness of doing academia. The freewriting activity takes thought for a walk. I don't know why the circlers underlined these particular words, but they resonate now and link back to some of the discomfort in the circle as a space of difference discussed in Chapter 1. It is a struggle for me to get the breath, rather than the theory-data correspondence of the conventional academic piece as I read these words in the freewrites. Freewriting is a stream of consciousness exercise, designed to tap into the thought flow where we feel the way hand, heart and head are interlinked. It does not feel right to look for themes that pre-exist in frameworks.

Natasha's words that 'sometimes doing academia is sore' send me sideways. While I am trying to analyse 'with soft eyes',[5] parallel to this moment of analysis, and to the circle, I am responding to students signed up for the free online course for postgraduates starting out on their research journey. Perhaps it's because of the way we have framed the course that so many participants have foregrounded their desire to write differently, to write with more 'joy' – the word comes up often – as an outcome for the course. Dare we hope for a sea change?

Yes, sometimes doing academia is sore, not just because of the publish or perish, mindless churning out for the factory of knowledge, salami-slicing, commodification. The soreness is there in the blog entries written by students on the online course. What if you're sick to your soul because of your inherited philosophy; or constantly walking a tightrope of too much or not enough involvement; or fighting so hard for legitimacy as a researcher, thinker, or professional, to be taken seriously; or stuck because, even as an engineer, you are encountering a fear of letting down your 'subjects'.

We have come a long way from laughter in isolation, restoring it to a more complex space, through a group inquiry.

Shaking the Tree

This exploration of laughter has shaken the tree of language and rather than simplifying the world, more concepts have come loose – defensiveness, trauma, shame, solace. In sharing this chapter with the circlers as part of the ethics process, Natasha remembered the feeling she had of writing something she shouldn't say – that perhaps there *wasn't enough* laughing in the circle. She took hold of this word, solace, saying that it is 'spot-on' and shared a recent experience of not being able to stop laughing and how disconcerting it had been.

All of us have at different times been ashamed or embarrassed around our writing. Shame and embarrassment are different: embarrassment more temporary, socially visible. As Goffman (1967: 112) says, with embarrassment, 'social structure gains elasticity; the individual merely loses composure'. Shame is a more long-term, enduring feeling of unworthiness, a feeling that lingers in private space, whereas embarrassment is short-lived. Perhaps…one of the things that the circle makes possible is that by diffracting writing into small segments and multiple readings – the two pages to be read by peers who are outsiders to the disciplinary discourse – we are regularly confronted with moments of embarrassment. But these moments, like micro-doses of nutrients or mind-expanding substances, are low-stakes. They give a window into shame, allowing a little light and air to enter into the opaque and lingering experience of feeling shame. Circlers often briefly lose composure, and then recover it, as they are regularly exposed to small moments of embarrassment. These moments are often talked about and named while we are together in the circle, in the process losing their disciplinary power. Perhaps people are sometimes saving *me* from embarrassment.

Shame has been in the background in this chapter on staying with the laughter. Ellen worried about it in her drawing: she is concerned that there's a pathology around writing that makes us wallow in the laughter. It pops up in my word 'bekvol', spitting out food in public, and in Tia's anger and shame at being complicit with racism in the circle. Perhaps it goes underground in some of the other freewrites, manifesting as silence. The point made by Elspeth Probyn that shame is a deeply relational form of embodiment and that within it lie possibilities for ethical action is expressed in her words in the interview with Viv Bozalek, Ronelle Carolissen and Tammy Shefer: she says, 'You cannot be ashamed if you are accused of something you don't care about' (Probyn *et al.*, 2019: 327).

Turning now to shame and writing, in 'Blush: Faces of Shame', Probyn (2005) argues that *of course* writing involves shame: 'It is interested, deeply embedded in contexts, politics and bodies' (2005: 162). How can we live up to this responsibility? She explores the writing of well-known authors who have written about shame, including Primo Levi for whom as a survivor of Auschwitz, 'shame enlarges the man'. It is everywhere. Postcolonial shame, that we either run backwards towards our masters or fall off the cliff. Pride/confidence may flicker briefly. Arguing for a shame-induced ethics of writing 'the spectre of not interesting readers and the constant worry about not adequately conveying the interest of our chosen topics should send a shiver down the spines of writers' (2005: 101). Questions about how we write without reinscribing the Anglocentric contours of the academy; how we write in ways that that do not reinscribe inequality or further underline masculinist ways of knowing, have to be kept alive. We have to keep trying. And laughing helps as we 'see ourselves' when frames mingle and collide. The small charges of affect, alternating between laughter, shame, and many other feelings can orient us towards a next feeling or thought or step that is less alienated than it might have been.

In the next chapter, I focus on the relationship between writing and time. Struggles to write – to be productive in the commodity sense of meeting deadlines for products that will go in the formal archive – mean that we are taking up time, while the clock is ticking. In regimes of capitalist performativity in the knowledge economy, failures to keep pace with the expectations of the clock are sources of deep discomfort and inadequacy. For many, this is a source of shame. 'One word at a time', says Stephen King (2008), that's the secret of his prolific writing. The next chapter will explore the relationship between writing and time to think about how writing-along-the-way may impact on the deeper, wider archive of memory practices in research, when 'should' becomes 'what if?' and 'maybe'…

Notes

(1) After Wilder Penfield and Theodore Rasmussen (1950), Montreal Neurological Institute, Montreal, Quebec, Canada. Online at https://neurostudyclub.mcgill.ca/jun2002/jun2002_p4.htm)

(2) The two-day workshop I attended was offered by the Cape Higher Education Consortium (CHEC), part of a suite of courses convened by Vivienne Bozalek on reconfiguring scholarship. Elmarie has published an article describing the process of running workshops on concepts at South African universities after the #RMF and #FMF protests. See Elmarie Costandius (2019), 'Fostering the Conditions for Creative Concept Development'.

(3) Freewriting is a well-travelled method associated with process pedagogy, made popular by the work of Peter Elbow (1998). It is a way of generating ideas and fluency, with the emphasis on the thought flow rather than on accuracy and correctness. It involves writing without interruption to edit or correct.

(4) The prompt is a phrase that everyone starts off with, so there is no hesitation about getting the writing started. Each writer will veer off on their own train of thought, resulting in varied, personal explorations.

(5) A phrase introduced by James Garraway in a workshop on how to analyse data in a CHEC workshop on writing research proposals. This is a reference to Detective Bunk in 'The Wire': 'You know what you need at a crime scene? Soft eyes. If you got soft eyes, you see the whole thing. You got hard eyes, you staring at the same tree, missing the forest'.

5 One Word at a Time: Finding Rhythm in Writing

Time is not a line in two equal directions [...] the secret of time lies in this slippage that we feel on our pulse, viscerally, in the enigma of memory, in anxiety about the future. This is what it means to think about time. What exactly is this flowing? Where is it nestled in the grammar of the world?

Carlo Rovelli (2018: 19-20) *The Order of Time*

The problem of time in writing is at the heart of this chapter. It begins with anecdotes from the circle that raise questions about the prevailing view of clock time in the university and in the lives of research writers. The chapter takes a step into re-thinking time and its relationship to the writing of research. I consider the relationship between clock time and the root metaphor in English of language as a conduit. The clock is always ticking loudly, marking and measuring, assumed to guarantee progress towards completion of the product. The stories about time and writing raise the importance of Aeon as lived, subjective time, as an important way of nudging Chronos – clock time – in a quest to experience a sense of flow. I explore the Given–New principle of communicative dynamism in knowledge structure as a way of thinking about how knowledge-making unfolds in writing.

One Word at a Time

A provocation from Stephen King, the prolific writer in the horror genre, frames this chapter. In this much-cited advice, he says, 'When asked, "How do you write?" I invariably answer, "One word at a time," and the answer is invariably dismissed. But that is all it is' (King, 2008: 17). One word at a time – so simple, and so complex. I deconstruct his advice to see what is hidden in it to try to find a life-affirming rhythm that can reveal what is underneath clock time with its schedules and deadlines. This rhythm can be felt in the comfort of writing together, quietly at workshops, writing retreats or in the Thursday circle. The soft clack of the keyboard, the sigh, the chuckle, the restless shift of a chair, the coffee mug gently returned to rest on the table, our thought-flows merging and diverging. This sense of immersive, suspended time seems to enable a different way of being-in-time that is less atomised and alienating than the commodified, regulated time of academic knowledge-making.

The advice that writing happens one word at a time suggests that it is easy to unfold from one word to the next. The slow unfolding of words over time creates sentences, which are the core material for paragraphs, chapters and for the making of knowledge itself. In this chapter I try to re-think the relationship between writing, time and knowledge-making in various ways drawn from ideas about writing as method explored in Chapter 2. I go beyond the circle at times, drawing more widely from courses and workshops that, together with the circle, make up a suite of writing support offerings at the University of Cape Town. These reflections on time are a response to overly mechanistic thinking about the linearity of writing as a progression towards the consumable at the end – the thesis or article that hides its history. Leander and Boldt (2013) call out this 'domestication' of literacy that comes with textual, rationalist approaches to reading and writing that are projected towards an inevitably convention-bound future product. They are interested in a non-representational approach to literacy-related action, 'not as projected towards some textual end point but as living its life in the ongoing present, forming relations and connections across signs, objects, and bodies in often unexpected ways' (2013: 13). This chapter considers what that literacy-related action might look like in relation to time and knowledge-making.

I begin with some of my reflections that illustrate the temporal complexity of the lives of researchers in the circle and how they express themselves in writing before I explore the relationship between time and divine discourse.

Time Stories from the Circle

The first two reflections were written in late 2017. Reflection 10 describes a circle where we all wrote together. If no-one offers to bring two pages, we arrange what we call a Just Write circle where we all, including facilitators, work quietly on our writing. 'Just write' is the term coined by our postgraduate scholars who resisted and rejected the term 'Shut up and write',[1] which is in widespread use internationally to describe this practice of writing together in timed bursts. The note reflects my enjoyment of the Just Write session. The room was full; we all wrote with a sense of common purpose and time flew by.

Reflection 10

Delighted that Ebba will be coming now that fieldwork is over – brings something special. I really enjoyed the Just Write session, and I could work on my book. Struggling for time. Lots of people – some vintages and some of Jo's students. The room feels full. Some with laptops, a few with notebooks and handwritten notes. Ebba is working on haikus to convince the sceptics in science 😊*. Kay sets the Pomodoro – 25 min – we have three sessions. Time goes fast. I'm so grateful to Jo for linking us up with her students. This gives us some more life. I was worried. But they'll be returning home for fieldwork soon.*

It is an unusual entry in that I was more focused on delight than on anxiety. I seldom made notes on comfortable or routine circles.

In the next entry I have chosen, there were very few students. I note that one scholar has to re-think her research because events, specifically the student protests, have overtaken her, moving faster than the pace of her knowledge-making in writing. I also notice that coincidentally, three people have talked about experiencing an 'itch' to write – a desire to keep the momentum going as the flow of writing has been interrupted.

Reflection 11

Today very small. Zo talks us through the backstory. Did her research before #RMF, will need to go back and re-interview.

3 times in 2 days, people describe separation from their work, and getting an itch to write, all mimed out. Zo is itching to write, so is Kamala (she was on holiday when her dad said 'No writing for two weeks!') and the student in yesterday's writing workshop for postdocs who said he started writing again when, after the earthquake, he had to relocate. He mimed getting itchy. Kamala talked about her 2 articles, both have been accepted but she doesn't want to submit. The timing doesn't feel right with the protests.

Zo's experience of being overtaken by events is a reminder that we need to be open to the reversals that happen as our writing struggles to keep up with the complexity of the world in which we write, and of which we are a part, as writing inserts us into the world again.

What catches my interest in the second part of this reflection is that the students who spoke of an itch to write express their desire to write in such positive terms. There is no procrastination or sense of blockage. These writers want to be reunited with the feeling of flow. This is felt in the body, on the skin – the interface between inside and outside – in the urgency of the now. I am struck by the coincidence of hearing postgraduate scholars speak of the itch to write but in thinking about it later, perhaps it is synchronous rather than coincidental in that I am attuned to their words. This is a moment when surface tension enters my thought again, a concept-in-action, it alerts me to what the postgraduate scholars are saying about the desire to get back to their writing.

The next reflection I include is written years later, during the pandemic. As mentioned in Chapter 1, Aditi offered the circle online through this time. No longer involved with the circle, but still included in the announcements with an open invitation to attend circles, I was interested in the regular weekly email from Aditi announcing that Thusi would be bringing two pages to the circle. I knew Thusi from the online research course I had developed with my colleagues.[2] She is introduced here and I return to her towards the end of this chapter in the section headed 'Don't leave yourself at the door!' where the activity we call the three circles exercise is described.

Reflection 12

I've been reading the weekly email announcements from Aditi – she says that Thusi is sharing a presentation on climate change. Can it be <u>our</u> Thusi? Aditi says, yes, she is preparing a presentation for her teacher training in the Netherlands! How did this happen? Last time we were in touch she was doing a PhD in Economics. I join the circle online, a bit late, pick up the end of a conversation on beekeeping and what it's like doing research in southern Africa. There are 7 people, they introduce themselves and their projects. I greet some as we know each other from other writing courses that I have facilitated. Thusi says she is still doing her PhD on social mobility and inequality, but that it's changed a lot, she is now doing it by publication [of three papers]. Thusi is recording this circle for fellow students to share. She runs through her presentation on climate change and is delighted when people in the circle critique the economic model used for its assumptions about development. 'I want them to see the limitations and it's great if it comes from the circle.' A week later, Thusi shares 2 pages from one of the papers she is writing for her PhD. It's a critique of an economist's argument about conspicuous consumption and racialised identity in South Africa. Thusi asks us: 'Am I making sense, do I come across as different from the author I am critiquing? And if you've stuff to add to bolster ...'. It's a strong critique that moves me and the circle responds warmly.

I am delighted that Thusi and I cross paths again. She has tapped in to the circle to create an assemblage for what she needs right now to support her thinking-writing journey.

Oscillating between the Clock and the Flow

While immersive flowing time is so alluring in that it carries us with it on a crest of becoming, a response to the itch to create, it is clock time that reigns in research production. Explanations for this go beyond neoliberal policies of speeding up and outsourcing. Research on metaphor in cognitive linguistics traces how abstract notions such as time and love are structured from a set of core domains grounded directly in experience, particularly around the experience of space. George Lakoff and Mark Johnson's *Metaphors We Live By* (1980) gives us some insight into how this works. A metaphor offers a frame for making sense that will privilege some meanings while obscuring others. Many of these metaphors sink back into language as dead or transparent images that become unmarked and normalised in everyday language over time. Two of the dominant unmarked metaphors that impact on knowledge-making are time as money ('I *spent* the whole day on one footnote'; 'It *saves* time if you use this software') and argument as war ('Those claims are *indefensible*'; 'The review was right *on target*'). These metaphors are so embedded that they are often not even noticed. Lakoff and Johnson wrote about this decades ago, before the regulatory regimes that structure academic work became so visible and problematic. These frames have been soaked up into discourse around writing and research.

The embedded frame of time-is-money is absorbed in the notion of the pipeline[3] as an image to structure thinking about postgraduate policy and support. In higher education, pipeline planning is a response to the lack of representativity, particularly of women, in the STEM disciplines. In South Africa the pipeline is mainly a solution to the serious problem of lack of transformation to right the historical injustices of apartheid exclusions from participation in higher education. The logic of the pipeline is an attempt to create a path from undergraduate through postgraduate, to academic work in the academy. It includes important initiatives like setting targets, finding funding, designing courses and timelines to address the lack of support for black postgraduates who may become academics. However, these good intentions are subject to the limitations of a reductive, managerialist approach to knowledge-making in which the power afforded to measurables over time plays into the broader discourse of managerialism in which there is a 'mania for assessment [...] an obsessive concern with the periodic and quantitative assessment of every facet of university functioning' (Mbembe, 2016: 31). The pipeline metaphor acts as a screen hiding the deeper issues of transformation and institutional culture, some of which were brought to the surface by the #MustFall protests.

The pipeline subsumes the writing of research in the conduit metaphor of communication (Reddy, 1979): spoken and written language are seen as a tube along which communication passes untroubled like a physical object from point a. (sender) to point b. (receiver). Writing lends itself to being counted in deliverables and citations, reinforcing the resilient ideology of academic writing as decontextualised skill (Boughey & McKenna, 2016; Lea & Street, 1998; Tuck, 2016). Examples of how dead metaphors create container-like frameworks of thought around communication are seen in phrases like '*put* your thoughts down', 'I didn't *get much from* the article', 'the ideas *come across* clearly'. These container metaphors tuck neatly into the pipeline. Struggles to write for whatever reason become leaks (wastage) in the system. Once the clock starts ticking, students measure themselves against this, frequently feeling they are out of synch with the official chronology as different allegiances and affect crowd in on the writing moment.

This sense of different layers of time being out of synch is described by Clement in this account of how he experienced time as a PhD student. As Clement got closer to the end of his thesis, he shared with friends in the circle that he had gone through a year of not writing at all while grieving the loss of a close family member. Years after completion of his PhD, Clement reflects in an email exchange between us on how he experienced time while writing his thesis, including periods when time 'froze':

> I experienced thesis writing time as a descent (or ascent?) into a different time zone – a slower time zone and sometimes, a *stillness* during which time *froze* – but not really, because 'exterior' time continued to move. So I am reminded of an animal trapped inside an iceberg – completely immobilized – but still aware that *it is* moving because the iceberg is carried forward by perpetual currents. The writers' circles helped to mediate this contradiction – of simultaneous movement and stillness [...] they reassured that the stillness was not really motionless because something – something related to the external time zone was *still moving*. So the trapped animal does not completely despair because it is aware that the iceberg is still moving – which means there are good chances it will eventually thaw.

His contributions to the circle as both facilitator and as a PhD student gave him the sense of moving-while-frozen, mediating between inner and outer time. Although he was not able to write during an extended time of grieving, regular useful engagement with the writing of others in a genuinely collaborative, rather than competitive way, enabled him to move while standing still, to be held in frozen time, while 'outside' time was felt as 'perpetual currents' rather than as a ticking clock. In addition to writing academically, Clement is also a poet and writes fiction where he innovates with layered time. In the email referred to above, he remembers 'once puzzling about time while feeling his way into a short story that I later just gave the title, St Augustine'.[4] In his role as both facilitator and participant, he brought this short story for us to read in the circle to encourage students to consider different kinds of writing. I remember the way time pulled in different directions at the surface of a richly heteroglossic text, from the opening line 'Chirombo died at the prime of his life, and stupidly too' to his post-death encounters with St Augustine where they meet in a 'reflectory' to ruminate on chronological and spiritual distance, time and space. The way Clement mixes and merges sacred and profane is a reminder of what Bill Ashcroft (2014: 76) calls 'knowing beyond meaning [...] as the thingness of the text unlocks a vast hermeneutic surplus [...] that exists beyond referentiality' in writing about time and epistemology in the postcolonial novel.

Clement's description of how he experienced PhD writing time alerts us to a world of possibilities in re-imagining time. Barbara Adam's notion of timescapes (2004) is useful, approaching time as both layered and spatial, enacted in the specificity of historical-material contexts, with different temporalities and rationalities operating at the same time, but foregrounded in different ways, as Adam unfolds in this comprehensive, compacted history of time. She identifies three pillars around which engagements with time form: time as tempering and transcendence; time as knowledge and know-how, and most importantly for us, time as colonization and control, a logic that is foregrounded in the industrial timescape and enacted in neoliberal policy landscapes (2004: 143–144).

There is a rich literature on the audited, time-is-money university and its impact on academic life. A special issue of the journal *Higher Education Research & Development* (HERD) is devoted to these themes 'and to how academics may practice their scholarship differently' (Peseta *et al.*, 2017). The way time is packaged out in relation to goals secured in the future becomes the perfect companion to the god view. When time is money, it functions as 'empty time', a core element in capitalist modes of production: '[T]to be first, that is faster than competitors, is crucial, and this applies whether the "product" is a new invention, garment, news story or a new drug' (Adam, 2004: 39). Empty time is future-oriented, disembedded, packaged, compressed and commodified as a mechanism to manage unruly futures from a point in the present. Adam also uses Colonisation with a capital C, in the historical-political sense of colonialism and its aftermaths. The notion of time and control is core in the colonial project, functioning as a principle of control and order that transcends place, to snare the Other in a way that makes sure people are perpetually behind while struggling to count as 'modern' or 'human' in the terms of the coloniser. Catherine Manathunga (2019) draws on Adams to ask important questions about the impact of hegemonic, assimilationist approaches to time on equity projects in Australia, showing how 'minority' students are further marginalised as they fail to thrive.

No wonder students took down the more prominent clocks in lecture halls during the #RMF and #FMF protests. Next I describe a moment from one of the courses I taught on during this time. The protests foregrounded time on the scale of the epoch – coloniality and postcoloniality – but also on a much smaller scale in how time measured in minutes binds our days to being productive.

In an intensive research writing course that we offered in 2015, it becomes clear how much clock time has harnessed our pedagogy. We have a tightly packed programme. It is the last day of what has been a stimulating and intense process of engaging with 25 postgraduates from different disciplines. Like the circle, it is a space of difference that needs its rituals to bind us all together. The day starts with students telling their research as story. Next is a session where students who are more advanced in their research journeys share their data guided by four generic questions we have honed over the years. We ask three students with different disciplines and methodologies to share their slides with the group. The clock is ticking. I feel intensely my duty to pace things responsibly. We need to get to the lunchbreak before our final session of writing together, followed by an evaluation of the course. Zanne is struggling to compress ideas in a presentation and the technology isn't working – the laptop won't speak to the screen. I can smell the delicious lunch that we will share on our last day together and am aware that the caterer needs to clear up by 2pm. Zanne is meticulous in taking us through this case study. She refers briefly to similar research on genocide. Patrick is angry, interrupting to challenge sources. You cannot cite that lawyer. There are people who have died for this issue and how it is interpreted. You have no right to say this! We look to the group for guidance. I can feel the final writing task after lunch slipping away and tell them about the students' protest with the removal of the clocks from lecture halls. Ana says, 'We need to stop the clocks'. So we do. We give time to this issue. The two continue with their heated dialogue that gradually softens as they explain and clarify. Patrick invites Zanne to come and visit the people he is writing about, if she still thinks the genocide case is relevant. We go to lunch late, and drastically shorten the final writing task, but not the evaluation. We decided to bend time, to allow time to balloon and flare out with the heat of this moment of knowledge-making, before it settles differently on the cool surface of the page.

In the heightened context of the protests, I become aware of how attached I am to the course timetable that has evolved over the years and to my investment in being on time and giving equal turns as a measure of respect. The timetable provides structure and ritual, but it also lassoes the future, as it embeds itself in what is ahead. Science operates in a similar way: 'Knowledge of the past is the basis on which the future is known and forged, foretold and foreclosed, on which innovation is justified and safety established' (Adam, 2004: 142). We have a crisis point in the Newtonian, measured and now commodified notion of time in contemporary institutions assisted by the compression of time with digital technologies, 'nowhere and now-here have become interchangeable' (2004: 146).

A parallel way of understanding time from a quantum physics perspective, alongside Newtonian objective, measured time, is described by Carlo Rovelli, theoretical physicist and popular science writer, in *The Order of Time* (2018). 'Empty time' crumbles with this understanding, becoming a phenomenon of situated inter-action, always relative to the event and to the viewer. At the subatomic level, everything is potentially connected in 'blurred' ways that we can't easily comprehend. In this quantum view, change is everything. It constitutes time:

> For millennia before clocks, our only regular way of measuring time had been the alternation of day and night [...] Diurnal rhythms are [...] essential to life, and it seems to me probable that they play a key role in the very origin of life on earth, since an oscillation is required to set a mechanism in motion. (Rovelli, 2018: 56)

To oscillate is to swing or sway, a moment of instability between things, a crossing of the midline for momentum and becoming. Rovelli feels that our available grammar struggles with this, privileging the *things* that make up the world rather than the *events* – the doing – happenings and processes that are by their nature impermanent (2018: 86). Positivist science wants to secure the relative permanence of things, perhaps in the face of the existential dread that a post-faith science opens up. In the previous chapter, I considered how nominalisation is good at building concepts and holding them still so they can transcend time and space. It is a story with nouns that is the bedrock of divine discourse. But the very long history of science foregrounds change, not stilling. Rovelli writes:

> The entire evolution of science would suggest that the best grammar for thinking about the world is that of change, not of permanence. Not of being, but of becoming. (2018: 86)

The next section takes this insight back to King's advice about one word at a time, that it might be a little less mechanical, more invested in a fertile becoming than in timeless being. This is a response to Rovelli's question posed in the epigraph that begins this chapter: 'What exactly is this flowing? Where is it nestled in the grammar of the world? ' (Rovelli, 2018: 19–20).

Between the Given and the New

With writing, it is the unfolding between micro and macro events – writing the words one at a time – that creates time. But grammar imposes some limitations on us. In academic writing, the preferred grammar reaches for a timelessness of classification as outlined in the discussion on nominalisation and how it anchors divine discourse in Chapter 3.

Perhaps the principle of communicative dynamism in linguistics can help to open this up. It might help to get closer to the grammar of becoming, rather than being, as a core principle, even in writing. Communicative dynamism is a way of thinking about the property of language that involves moving information forward. It is attributed to Jan Firbas (1971) and the Prague School of Linguistics, taken further in Michael Halliday's (1985) influential systemic functional grammar to develop a theory of the utterance as experienced by both speaker and audience. The Given–New principle is an element of communicative dynamism, the Given being the part of the utterance that is presumed known to the hearer while the New is the information that is experienced by the hearer as 'news'. The Given usually comes first, followed by the New. This Given–New principle of communicative dynamism is a key element in creating a working common sense to be shared in utterances.

The Given–New principle could be generative in raising awareness of research writing as it is relevant on different scales: at the level of the clause, sentence, paragraph and chapter, we are constantly shuttling between familiar and new insight. It is also a metaphor for knowledge-making itself, particularly for the PhD in which we are expected to 'contribute to knowledge'. What is new has to be carefully unfolded across thousands of words and hundreds of pages. I have tried this unfolding in the circle and in workshops in a call and response that begins at the level of the sentence and goes something like this: Let's start a sentence with 'The boy'... We all form an image of a boy of some kind. That is our Given, the point of departure. And a verb to follow? Participants often say 'kicks' or 'kicked', perhaps a memory from a Reader in the early years of schooling? Now we are starting to unfold the New. What do you want to come next? '...the ball' is a stock answer. So that's our New. How do we start the next sentence? 'He', 'The ball' or 'It...' We note the New of the first sentence has become the Given of the sentence under construction. '...flew over the wall and smashed the window'.

So we have gone from 'the boy' to 'the window' in a series of chained Given–New moves. This seemingly trivial exercise generates interesting discussion. What role do convention and ideology play in the way our sentences unfolded? We explore more examples, students look at their own writing, or try to work with a difficult piece of text they are struggling with at the moment by breaking it down into a series of chained Given–New pairings. The things – the Given and New elements – are set in motion by an oscillation between them – a verb.

One of the challenges with research writing is that the point of departure for the Given–New keeps changing depending on where the researcher is in the process and who the audience is. This is illustrated in some of the journal notes at the beginning of this chapter, in Zo's need to update her research in the context of the protests and in Bella's search for a concept that is not yet in the medical textbooks (Reflection 9 in Chapter 3). This is particularly challenging in writing an introduction to a thesis.

Reflection 13

We look at Sonja's intro. She's re-written it a lot – included much more personal stuff – including how the student protests have brought out a need to justify her stance. I am uncomfortable with how angry she sounds. Encourage her to include something on class and gender. Paul makes an interesting comment on reading Sonja's more personal, reflexive stuff – should you be foregrounding yourself? Are you more important than your research subjects?

What comes first – the point of departure – depends on which conversation you are in, and this changes through the research process. Thinking of writing spaces as spaces of difference, an obvious point in the writers' circle, but increasingly in postgraduate disciplinary and inter-disciplinary spaces, what is assumed to be common knowledge is going to be either formulaic or contested.

Another grammatical affordance Rovelli (2018) identifies that has consequences for science practices is indexicality, 'the characteristic of certain words which have a different meaning every time they are used, a meaning determined by where, how, when and by whom they are spoken.

Words such as "here", "now", "I", "this", "tonight" all assume a different meaning depending on who utters them and the circumstances in which they are uttered' (2018: 133). Jakobson called these shifters (1971). 'In every experience, we are situated within the world' (Rovelli, 2018: 134). As Donna Haraway's (1988) embodied objectivity and situated knowledge tell us, we are always seeing from within the world, from a particular point of view. So Sonja's I is a shape-shifter. It's not time that's changing, it is the student researcher that is changing. Paul's question to Sonja – are you more important than the people you are researching? – is profound. By foregrounding the I, there is a shift in subjectivity and Paul is not sure he likes it. 'We can only think of a single time, the time of our experience' (Rovelli, 2018: 171). But this single time isn't unified, clearly demarcated, can only be experienced in the thickness of the now. And yet grammatically we are tied to absolute distinctions between past, present and future.

What does this mean for research writing? We are invited to experiment with time and the oscillation between the Given and the New in as many ways as possible to breathe new life into the surface of the language in which we write our research. Formulae and recipes for writing will only get us so far.

'Don't leave yourself at the door!'

The kinds of process activities that we do in the writers' circle and writing workshops – writing along the way rather than 'the write-up' – become important as alternatives to a dependence on formulaic recipes for writing. At some point, again prompted by issues raised by students during the protests, students were welcomed to teaching spaces with the invitation, 'Don't leave yourself at the door'. There are many ways to do this, one of which is freewriting, described in Chapter 4 as a method to engage writers in the thought-flow. Another is the Just Write sessions that we adapted for our online writing courses, when students wrote in timed bursts synchronously, separate in space but not in time. Writers can be them/ourselves in an embodied way. One of the interesting things about activities like Just Writes and freewriting is that they are premised on brief spells of clock-time that are broken down into minutes rather than months and years. This is similar to the strategy of working on what Kamler and Thomson (2006) call tiny texts[5] – working on bite-size chunks of text that can help unlock bigger arguments, pages, chapters and manuscripts. One word at a time is invited in a freewriting activity when you try to follow a stream of consciousness and don't diverge from the page to look up a reference. While these activities mess with time and provide an ego-less space, they don't directly address the problem of the grammar of the world which as Rovelli (2018) identifies, is not up to the complexity of how for the writer, the time of experience meets clock time in the pipeline.

A common activity that engages the simultaneity of past, present and future inviting subjectivity in the writing moment is what we call the three circles exercise. It is an adaptation of an activity designed by Sharman Wickham, a research development consultant who taught on one of the courses in the suite of writing courses for postgraduates. Sharman bases the activity on Linda Shepherd's *Lifting the Veil: The Feminine Face of Science* (1993) which describes research about doctoral students who complete their theses well and recall it as a positive experience. For this to happen, there has to be some sort of 'psychic energy', the productive inter-action (but not necessarily alignment) of three contextual spheres: the personal (our biography and interests and abilities that come with our first family and early socialisation); the social (community, historical events that impact on the work, and professional – the questions we ask every day in our working lives); the theoretical (the conceptual resources and frames that we have developed over time, and those that we have for this particular project as well as those we need in the future).

The task pitches students into thinking about time on multiple levels: childhood influences, ongoing personal commitments and doubts, socio-political events, past and present as well as projections into the future. For some students, the three circles exercise is a point of crisis as they face their doubts about their commitments to their research. The multiple spheres also engage the thought-flow in the moment of sitting down with pen in hand, knowing that there will be a chance to edit what you would like to put out there in writing.

In workshops and circles, we ask students to jot down notes and then draw a cluster of circles, with each circle representing a contextual sphere, before talking or writing about their circles with a wider audience. The drawing is another transmodal moment that takes them out of prose. They play around with the relative size of the circles and the position of each circle in relation to the others. Typical patterns are three nesting circles, where the theoretical circle is rarely the larger, outer circle; or intersecting circles, like a Venn diagram, but where students experiment with the relative size and position of their circles (Figure 5.1).

Sometimes students seem to hit the sweet spot of three more-or-less equivalent, overlapping or nesting circles. More common is a more dynamic, unstable representation where the circles are different in size, and differently related to one another, sometimes with no overlap. Often the theoretical circle is smaller, less established, and sometimes it does not overlap with the personal and social spheres at all. There is no equilibrium but there is a dynamic, a 'next'.

There are moments I recall, helped by having jotted down brief notes. One stands out for me from the circle. I did not see her drawing, but when Vuyo talked about her circles when we did the exercise in the circle, she spoke of the dissonance between her personal and theoretical circles. In her personal circle, faith and religion were important, but in her

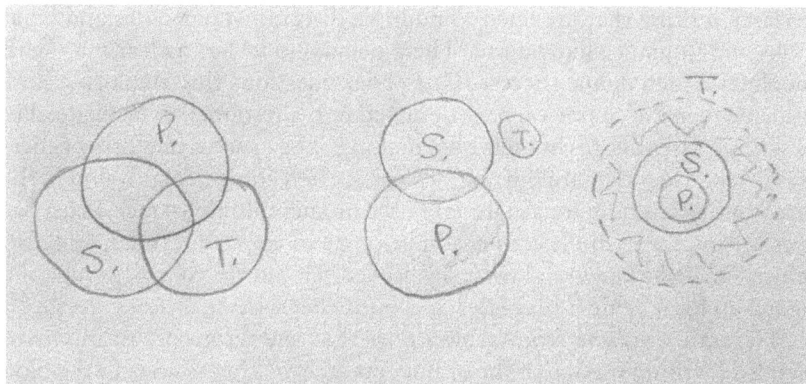

Figure 5.1 Typical patterns for how students arranged the spheres (Personal, Social and Theoretical) for the three circles exercise

discipline, religion may be used as an indicator of psychosis. She has to navigate this contradiction. I also recall when Ayanda spoke of the struggle to both connect and separate his circles. He is passionate about the nexus between nature conservation and land reform and the potential tensions between these. He wants both to 'win'. But his personal connection to social justice and land reform goes deep because of forced removals in the 1970s which shaped his growing up. When communities dispossessed under apartheid make claims to land in areas considered to be important for biodiversity, they hardly get taken seriously or awarded any rights. When he tried to write objectively, he felt he was being disingenuous. Another example that I remember was in a workshop for PhDs researching food security and governance, when some participants came up and drew their circles on the whiteboard. For one person, the circles were concentric, with the personal in the middle, the social around it, and a circle representing the theoretical sphere lightly drawn on the outside with a thin zigzag line 'because it is dynamic, always changing, and definitely less important than the inner circles. I've always believed that the personal is political, and my theory is generated from that insight' (see example in Figure 5.1). For these students, when they bring themselves in, there is no clear separation of past, present and future.

Exploring the Three Circles

The focus in the rest of this chapter reverts to Thusi, the PhD student we met earlier in this chapter, who used the three circles exercise during two iterations of the online Journeys in Research Writing course. This account is based on analysis in our paper, 'I am everywhere all at once': Pipelines, rhizomes and research writing' (Samson et al., 2021) where we introduce the rhizome alongside the pipeline, to argue for approaches to research writing that are open to multiple directions, outcomes and what looks at first glance like failure. The pipeline model has a clear map with timelines which define success. Our paper questions this, exploring how students turn the course we have designed into a resource, to be plugged in to writing assemblages of their own making. The process of writing generates assemblages that are shifting, strategic, often going underground in the discovery of serendipitous material in the moment. In this paper Thusi figures in how she used the course as a resource to connect, extend, and also refuse. Once she had found what she needed, she left the course, though she signed up for it again a year later to energise her writing process afresh.

Here are extracts from a blog post that she wrote on an intensive blended learning version of the online research writing course. In the blog reflection, she introduced herself on the first day after a day of grappling with what knowledge looks and feels like:

> My presence on this course obviously signals that I did change my mind about completing a PhD, but that is only because I have decided that for me knowledge generation is going to look different. So while knowledge in my field tends to be equations and numbers, I want to move the equations to the background and allow the text/story/narrative to take centre stage. Wish me luck!

After working on the three circles exercise, students go back to their blogs and write in response to this prompt, 'Thinking about the circles today, I am learning…'. Extracts from Thusi's blog post are included below:

> 'Thinking about the circles today, I am learning…'
>
> … that the personal is much bigger than I once thought. I cannot erase myself from the research that I am doing. I am a black female and my unique lived experience stemming from my blackness and my female-ness will always find itself in my research whether I intentionally put it into my writing piece or not. I can never leave me off the pages of my research because even my choice of topic stems from my 'me-ness'.
>
> Today I realised that the reason I decided to study social mobility stems from my childhood and how my cousin and I used to play together as little girls and how I now realise that we belong to different socioeconomic classes and how our mothers – sisters – also belonged to different socioeconomic classes. […]
>
> This personal example feeds into my research interest which is social mobility in Soweto. How can a group of people who initially all started off on the same economic footing, with the same history and ethnicity have such different socioeconomic outcomes 23 years into democracy.
>
> The personal is currently looming large in my research thinking, but I think it is because not only is the personal personal, but it is also political. So the two circles: personal and economic/social/political are very similar and so seem like to be taking up a lot of room.

> The circle that I have not spent enough time on is the theoretical framework. I think the reason for this is because I thought I 'knew' the theory in my field. The theory is that in South Africa the answer to any inequality question is 'education' and 'the legacy of apartheid'.

She explores this idea about education as an explanation for sustained inequality, generating a series of questions that take her to this:

> Actually I am sick and tired of hearing about the education theory. I think we are hiding behind it. Education is extremely complex and it takes years to make it through the system to see whether any educational interventions have made a difference. I suspect that education is a catch-all for connections and contacts. It is not so much education but what contacts education introduces you to that makes the difference [...].

Thusi takes up this opportunity through the three circles exercise to bring herself in to the writing process in a way that we see writing 'as a form of thinking, rather than as a conduit for thought external to the text' or something that follows it (Hanley, 2019: 414). Seeing writing in this way enables the writer to go beyond the absolute separation of past, present and future, and to explore the pronoun I as a shifter, incorporating a relationship to a we and a they.

Reading this text through the lens of Leander and Boldt (2013: 13), as 'living its life in the ongoing present, forming relations and connections across signs, objects, and bodies in often unexpected ways', reading for 'something more' (2013: 13), something else happens. The question is less 'How has Thusi represented her life as biography?' than 'How does the act of writing create assemblages that constitute becoming and an emergent self?'.

Working with the three circles activity, personal, social and theoretical can touch each other with unexpected outcomes. There are many places for the Given and the New to be explored. The tasks like the three circles and their product submitted seem to interact in a smudging where it tells us little to try and separate process from product. Words are paths towards a next in which the pressure of hegemonic ways of knowing, being and doing that insist on policing the line between messy process and neat product can be challenged. By stalling a representational approach to the analysis of Thusi's encounter with the three circles and staying with her writing right where it is, the godview is dislodged for a moment, to offer a glimpse of the 'hermeneutic surplus' (Ashcroft, 2014) that opens up beyond a focus on representation alone.

'Working against the stultifying effects of duration'

This exploration of the three circles resonates with Claudia Lapping's work (2017) in which active researchers were asked to free-associate using the prompt 'Say something about the text that you have chosen' for discussion in the research interview in which she is interested in how future orientation plays out in research practice. Lapping identifies three different temporalities that constitute academic subjectivities in research practice: empty, decontextualised chronological temporalities; teleological temporalities – references to disciplines, methods, canonical texts that like chronological time, pre-exist; and most interesting, a 'cobwebby' temporality that is narcissistic, suspended, nurturing, in which, in a Deleuzian/Guattarian reading,[6] there is a build-up of 'amassed potential connections' (2017: 917) in which there are political possibilities for bringing forth a 'new':

> [t]he 'new' might be brought into being by varying the habitual rhythmic interplay between existing temporalities of academic practice. To do this, the animating but also stultifying effects of duration must be replaced by the affective capacities of desire, a shift frequently associated with aesthetic modes of intervention, but also with the organism's incomplete but developing awareness of its complex and multifaceted relations to other bodies. (Lapping, 2017: 919)

In replacing the 'stultifying effects of duration' with the 'affective capacities of desire' Lapping sees potential for new spaces that invite this kind of suspended time. This creates possibilities for emergent meanings to appear, and be shared, away from those chronological and disciplinary spaces occupied by an 'explicit sense of futurity' (2017: 917).

Her paper helps to explain how textwork in spaces such as those described in this chapter – the writers' circle, Just Write sessions, retreats, courses – allow something else to happen alongside the disciplinary and pipeline temporalities that drag us towards a normative *should,* by making it possible to surface a *might be.* Alternating speaking and writing, and exploring the aesthetic modes of drawing, poetry, fiction writing, invite a recursive, in-the-moment relationality that is more than the sum of its parts. Activities like the three circles exercise mess with time by engaging simultaneity rather than sequence. They enrich the possibilities for growing new audiences and ways to start and then unfold a text one word at a time, but from a different Given towards a possible unthought New, that can become a new Given.

Surely this is what new knowledge is about?

Notes

(1)   As part of a course development process, we convened a group of postgraduate students to trial the online research writing course Journeys in Research Writing that my colleagues and I were developing. Several of the students were from the Thursday circle. We wanted to introduce a synchronous writing session, as imagined in the global Shut up and Write movement. The term Shut up and Write was coined by Inger Mewburn in the popular blog, The Thesis Whisperer. When our colleagues in the School of Education set up a similar weekly writing space for their postgraduates,

students also resisted the term Shut up and Write and called the forum Thula Ubale meaning 'ssh (or hush) and write' in isiXhosa. See Soraya Abdulatief and Xolisa Guzula (2018) for more about their writing forum.

(2) Thusi was in my thoughts as I had just been writing about her as a research participant on a course that we analyse in our paper, Sean Samson, Catherine Hutchings, Taahira Goolam-Hoosen and Lucia Thesen (2022). No longer responsible for the circle, my note is extensive as I write her into this book in the new context of the writers' circle.

(3) There are lots of references to the pipeline in the titles of articles. Here are a few extracts from titles: 'How can we strengthen the academic pipeline?'; 'A leak in the academic pipeline'. Chaya Herman's article 'Expanding Doctoral Education in South Africa: Pipeline or Pipedream?' (2011) is a strong critique of the notion of the pipeline in discourse about doctoral education locally.

(4) This short story is published in *Writing Now: More Stories from Zimbabwe,* edited by Irene Staunton (2005).

(5) Pat Thomson illustrates the use of tiny texts in her blog at https://patthomson. net/2022/09/19/academic-writing-from-tiny-text-to-road-map/ where she describes how these tiny texts also cheat time.

(6) In data analysis in this paper, Claudia Lapping (2017) contrasts this Deleuzian/ Guattarian reading with a Lacanian interpretation to see how each unfolds a political potentiality. I am focusing on the former.

6 Punctuating the Flow: Reflections from Beyond the Circle

More meetings today so this feels unfinished but it's a draft 😊.
This made me realise that in a sense, writing is always a train of thought, interrupted for publication.

(Ronelle Carolissen, in personal communication, email sharing a draft with participants on a workshop)

This chapter engages three writers who had been present in the circle as doctoral students. Interviews with Kay, Siwela and Tia, years after completion of their PhDs, involve a retrospective look at the circle and how it featured (or not) in their writing lives. The idea of punctuation holds this chapter together. I use it in different ways, most importantly with reference to Barthes' (1981) *punctum* as intense, subjective piercing in responding to data, with the understanding that the written word cannot catch up with, or represent, the affect that saturates the present. The moments of punctum in the interviews suggest layers of intense feeling where the numbing effects of the long duration of thesis writing may be overturned and transformed.

While doing the interviews for this chapter, it became clear that I could not isolate the past in any reliable way. The texts created in our interaction must also be read through the events of the research process described in this book, as a 'concrete encounter with the real' (St Pierre, 2019: 12), alongside and at times displacing the conventional apparatus of qualitative research methods. The elements of qualitative research are here: the way the interviews were set up, recorded and transcribed, as well as the use of archival emails and discussions, and some of the analysis is in this spirit. I am torn between the world, the book and the author (Deleuze & Guattari, 1987: 27). I move between them in a way that initiates a process of interference on the surface which is more than the sum of its parts. The research process creates something more than the intended aims and objectives allow. In the spirit of post-qualitative inquiry, something unintended happens that wasn't there before, as I try out concepts to re-orient thinking (St Pierre, 2018). The research technologies of email, recordings and transcriptions are brought together in the thickness of the present and uncertainty of the future, re-made in the writing process through the researcher–ex-supervisor–friend–facilitator relationship with ex-circlers in a way that brings out ripples that inaugurate new enactments. This 'affective attunement' (Gibbs, 2015) is discussed more fully in Chapter 3.

Punctuation

Ideas in this chapter are woven around different but related meanings of the word punctuation. As Theodore Adorno and Shierry Weber Nicholsen (1990: 305) say in the context of writing poetry, punctuation is a reminder of what writing can only fail to include – voice and breath. It renders breath in these slightly comical ciphers reminding us of our attempts to reconcile the difference between speaking and writing. To punctuate in the grammatical sense is to discipline speech by offering spacing to differentiate between words, marks such as exclamation marks, dashes, question marks and the humble comma, to give us resting spaces lest speech crowd us out altogether. While punctuation brings the spoken word to order, it also offers an essential resource to translate speech into something meaningful for the reader across time and distance, a metamorphosis from raw sound with embodied accent and affect, into something that can be shared.

A second meaning lies beyond grammar: to punctuate is to mark a resting point – a pause in something that is unfolding in time, between something that came before, and something that is to come. The circle seemed to serve as a way of punctuating the undifferentiated flow of things in the students' research journey: as Kay says in her interview in this chapter, the circle offered her 'nice regular stitches'. Similarly any completed textual product such as a thesis or article is a moment of punctuation in the flow of a life that includes writing.

A third meaning comes from the Latin roots of punctuation – from *punctus* and *pungere*, to prick or pierce, puncture or wound. Roland Barthes (1981) draws on this meaning in the concept of punctum as the personally poignant detail in a photograph which 'pierces' or 'pricks' a particular viewer, constituting a subjective meaning unrelated to any cultural/discursive consensus, which he calls the studium. The punctum is an element of an image that 'rises from a scene, shoots out of it like an arrow' disturbing the official meaning 'for punctum is also: sting, speck, cut, little hole—and also a cast of dice. A photograph's punctum is that accident which pricks me (but also bruises me, is poignant to me)' (1981: 26–27). While it is a feature of the moment in the act of communication – the moment of taking the photograph or in this case recording the interview – it only reveals itself afterwards. Being together in the interview or in writing an email, we may not think these moments are important. They only come to light/life later, in looking at the photograph or the transcript and living with it. Thus the punctum is always in-between, in movement between an initial event and the next interpretive event.

Punctum is a reminder of subjective time. It is Aeon, what Deleuze and Guattari (1987: 26) call 'the indefinite time of the event, the floating time [...] a simultaneous too-late and too-early, something that is going to happen and has just happened'. Aeon is felt as a simultaneous movement in two directions, opening to the past and to the future, 'a time that retreats and advances, divides endlessly into a proximate past and an imminent future' (Reynolds, 2007: 155). Deleuze (2004) wants to empha-sise Aeon for its transcendental possibilities, over the normative time of Chronos, which tells about bodies, states of affairs, accountability and causality. The first two meanings explored – punctuate as in disciplining speech and as in marking a pause – seem to me to stitch Aeon to Chronos. Both are needed to be in the world, but we need more of the transcendent and transformative possibilities that Aeon offers.

An Inquiry into the Mesh of Things

After an initial individual approach to the three ex-circlers – Kay, Siwela and Tia – I emailed them together, saying that I was 'interested in how you found what you needed to take you to completion, to explore that idea of a network or mesh of "things" with you three in order to think more broadly about an alternative postgraduate writing pedagogy'. The circle was one element in the mesh of things, freighted in different ways for each person. As a precursor to the interviews, I asked them to respond in writing to focal activities that included a brief description of their research focus, and a depiction of the 'ecology' in which they had written their theses – the groups, individuals, places, spaces, texts, emotions, resources, policies – that enabled them to finish. They could do this as an image (diagram, map), table, written text or combination. This was fol-lowed by a question about where and how the circle fitted in to their description of the mesh of things.

At the time of the interviews, Kay had just arrived in Berlin to take up a project lead position in a large research collaboration. As she was in the throes of packing up to leave Cape Town, she wasn't able to send me the written piece I had requested so all comments are drawn from her inter-view. Siwela was in Johannesburg from where he works as a lecturer at South Africa's large open distance learning university in nearby Pretoria. He joined the circle while on sabbatical in Cape Town towards the end of his PhD. Tia had started a postdoc in Cambridge and I was in Cape Town. I chose to work with them as I knew all three relatively well. Tia and Kay joined the circle early in their PhD processes, remaining in the circle for a while after graduation. Siwela had been my PhD student. I hold each person in high regard. Our paths continue to cross beyond the circle.

I had asked them to look back at the circle from where they were at the time of working together on this inquiry. How they remember the circle will be shaped by their current circumstances, their journeys since the circle, as well as their relationships to me as ex-facilitator and supervisor. There isn't anything pure that can be retrieved, distilled and described once and for all. The occasion of our contact through this research process, first with the written piece and then the follow-up interview, sets up a kind of turbulence as we move between past and future. The interview becomes a portal for bringing what is inside to the surface where it can be shared in a process that is part of life's flow. Like the circle, the interview creates a new event, a living interface between inside and outside.

This sense of life as ongoing is evident in a literal way in that all three are re-making their intellectual journeys. Siwela's interests seem to me to have expanded substantially beyond his PhD, embracing as much as he can to widen and deepen sociolinguistics. Both Tia and Kay had been in uncertain and at times precarious work situations, moving between post-docs and projects in areas adjacent to their PhDs. All three have to work hard to keep faith with what really matters in their disciplinary, broader intellectual and personal projects.

The feeling I have in listening to the interviews, reading the transcripts and the written pieces, is of a flow, like water from a spring or lava from a volcano, a sort of inside-out movement that does not want to be held still. It actively resists stilling and fixing. The main question (if there is one) is not, what did the Thursday circle mean to you? (though that is important), but the more interesting questions are: how is the circle remembered as part of something bigger? Who are we at this moment of becoming? How are different temporalities at play here? How is meaning possible at all? What does this inquiry suggest for imagining doctoral writing differently? The first question is subsumed by the subsequent questions.

I move now to the specificity of interaction with each person. The three scholars are introduced below through their PhD projects. When I asked them to describe their research, they knew that there could be no guarantee of anonymity: even if they chose pseudonyms, their projects and disciplines would make them identifiable.

'The research topic in PhD life'

In the interview, Kay describes her focus on India's role in climate change at the intersection of the disciplines of Political Studies and International Relations (IR), locating the PhD in an ongoing commitment to 'what really interests me':

> Well the research topic in PhD life was India's role over 22 years in the climate change negotiations, but specifically looking at it from a Critical International Relations point of view. Part of the reason I did it that way was to try and bring the different disciplinary areas together, because a

lot of the climate change focused writing I had found wasn't really steeped in a conceptual framework or in a theoretical box or anything like that. And when I read the International Relations literature, bizarrely enough, even though from my point of view climate change is the most important international relations topic of all times, most of the writers in the IR world didn't really like, weren't engaged much with climate change as a topic. Some part of it was an attempt to bring those literatures to a point where they might at least overlap at some point, and part of it was to provide a kind of consensual IR thinking to an issue in the climate change world. So, I suppose, that is the part that really interests me, how is it that nations with very different ideas and very different motivations all manage to work together. It is a, what do you call it, like a global commons problem, but that is not quite the right term.

Siwela's PhD was in Applied Language and Literacy Studies – an analysis of the discursive tensions in literacy practices for members of the South African Police Service (SAPS) who undertake a professional master's degree while in police service:

The final title of my thesis was 'When Police Become Postgraduates: An Intertextual Analysis of Research Proposals in the MTech Policing Degree at an ODL University'. The title changed and the focus was on following a group of MTech students over the process of writing the proposals, and using ethnographic framing to explore their own literacy practices and what they expressed through their writing, while paying attention to the fact that these texts were already accepted and somewhat valued within the system or culture of the academy from the point of view of a police professional on the way to attaining a master's degree.

Tia's thesis in Sociology was about stigma and waste pickers:

Waste pickers are the people who work informally, sifting through household refuse before the municipal truck arrives to empty it. I was looking at how stigma surfaces in their everyday interactions while working, how they managed the impression that others formed of them, and how negative stereotypes related to their ability to improve their working conditions. I worked with a group in Cape Town, once a week for a year, 'shadowing' my key informant who I positioned as my boss.

In the circle, we had shared accounts of Kay's field trip to India, Tia's weekly fieldwork with informal reclaimers on the streets of Cape Town, and Siwela's field trips to interview ex-students on the MTech in Policing in their work settings across the country. Each description above is inflected by the research conversation we are in now. Kay talks about her research project 'in PhD life' – that was then, but here I am now. Siwela talks about 'the final title', hinting at a series of changes that occurred during the process, knowing that as his supervisor, I would share memories of the process. In an inversion of the usual roles, Tia positions her key informant, a waste picker, as her 'boss'. This way of assigning roles to those who were part of her project emerges again in the interview described later. Kay's verbal account is longer, and different, with shifts in tense ('part of the reason I did it that way', 'that is the part that really interests me'), evaluation 'bizarrely enough' and a search for the right word ('I suppose, not quite the right term'). In the transcription, I can hear the sound of her voice, feel the relationality of our co-talking, as she gives an account of her research interests and history, her impatience with the mainstream in a quest for intellectual belonging.

Footing: Alignment to Ourselves and Others

A feature of the interviews is the addressivity, the relational sense that we know each other and are adjusting our speaking selves to the situation in which we find ourselves. Goffman (1981) calls this footing – the alignment or stance of participants to talk. A change in footing implies change in 'the alignment we take up to ourselves and the others present as expressed in the way we manage the production or reception of an utterance' (1981: 128). Goffman's footing is agentive in its emphasis on what is a largely conscious process of impression management. Notions such as intersubjectivity have a different emphasis that shifts the focus from individual agency to a structural, often unconscious and inevitable taking in of the other in all discourse. Working with the transcripts, I selected utterances where this taking in of the intersubjectivity of the interview with me seemed to be most strongly at work in for example a confessional tone or sharing of in-jokes. Below some of these utterances have been sampled from the interviews, mixed together in a collage and not attributed to any of the three speakers. I wanted a way of thinking about the interviews in general, without anchoring inside jokes, asides, confessions to any one person, or to the overt focus of the interviews: the writers' circle in the flow. In this way I was also trying to foreground a sense of emergence. I tried to work against the notion of fixed identities, self-contained bodies and causality in the interviews, and instead to try to be in the moment but without attribution.

I suppose I have to confess I am not a natural writer.

If there is such a thing – haemorrhaging time, and it really, I am afraid I am time conscious.

Maybe it is because English is not my first language.

I was pretty fine to just trust you, you know me, so you know if you write something, oh my god they will hit the roof, you will know!

But I got the impression that it was something you wanted to do, and no matter how busy you were, or you weren't, it always happened every week, you know. Rain or shine.

Because everyone knows that the actual creative stuff and interesting things are at the edges of your discipline, right?

Even intellectually, a bit more liberated, and that has really been my interest for a long time.

I was watching one of those digital natives when I was in Hong Kong, you said I should tell you about that.

Tell her a lot more is going on in my head.

I owe you breakfast.

The utterances have been loosely stitched together, roughly sequenced to express different kinds of footing: confessional, transactional, solidarity building, continuity or change. The new arrangement messes with the punctuation offered by the flow of speech in the interview. The I changes throughout, resulting in the emergence of a composite I that is changing footing all the time: asking for a fair reading, hearing an apology, sharing as a disciplinary or political insider, picking up a previous conversation, looking back and forwards, sharing gossip to build solidarity. This offers a context for reading the rest of the data from the interviews and written responses from the three researchers. It de-essentialises the people I am interviewing, creating instead a kind of background hum for the event, attuning both writer and reader to the emergent qualities in the interview as event.

The Circle in the Flow

In this section I consider what each person said about the circle, in the context of the broader environment of which it was a part. I move between conventional qualitative humanist research and a more experimental emergent approach. I have done so throughout this book as no one methodological or philosophical approach felt adequate for this account of the richness and complexity of this circle over time. So faithful recreations of circle memories and their location are important, but they are displaced as I enter the interview as an event 'in the middle' and try to create a new description, which itself becomes an event that can help us to think differently about how things might be in future. While I focus on the circle in the flow, I also find the moments of punctum. These are the moments that pierce me, stop me in my tracks in working with data. Maggie MacLure (2013) calls this 'data that glows', tugging on affect, asking for a different kind of attention. These moments are entangled in the relations between data and researcher, and do not sit outside of our interaction during these interviews. They are emphasised through the use of italics in the transcripts below, drawing attention to affect, to intense feeling, stumbles and stammering in language (as in Kay's *'what would you call it? like meh, words'*).

'Nice regular stitches' and 'the year in the swampland': Kay

The interview with Kay is as much about catching up as it is about the circle. Kay uses her laptop camera to show me round her flat and we look at the Berlin skyline together from her balcony. She describes her long search for the right work that will blend her skills and her politics. All her research jobs since graduating have chopped up this longed-for intellectual work in time and space. She was always given what she calls the Southern segment (India, South Africa), and was frustrated by having to slot what she saw and heard into a pre-ordained package that erased history and allocated the same shape and size to all geopolitical spaces. We share the irritation and humour of the Southern scholar and her difficulty with not 'really been able to leverage any of my knowledge to create a systematic niche for myself'.

We move on to her experience of writing the PhD, which she describes as a 'mixed bag', mainly 'hellish' with small hops of positive momentum as she grappled with a 'well-honed critical inner voice, so severe'. The PhD is a 'bizarre process, but I'm glad I did it' – at least, 'I'm glad it's over!'. I ask how the circle fitted in to this strange process:

> I needed the regular check in. And because my supervisor and I had a complex relationship, as she was also my boss, and she wasn't going to be the… And ja, it was just really, skeleton is OK, but it is not quite, now I am thinking of a tapestry, it was like the stitches that kept the part of my writing life together. Like nice regular stitches. Which were essential, you know. Like if I missed one or two it would be OK.

The 'nice, regular stitches' echo the ritual elements touched on in the description of the circle in Chapter 1. Given the radically open pedagogy of the circle, it was important that there was a regular meeting time, that the circle wouldn't collapse if anyone was absent, that we facilitators wouldn't take it personally if anyone missed a session. This regularity offered a refrain, a chance to do the same thing again, but knowing that each repetition was also a new iteration.

We knew before the interview that we would talk about what Kay had called her swamp year when she had been stuck. Parts of the recording aren't clear at this point in the interview as Kay is doing something else as we talk – washing up, clearing – and this muffles the emotion in her voice. There are tears and laughter. It feels wrong and invasive to be trying to transcribe the interview as she is asked to go to a painful emotional place:

> L: Also because you gave me that term, the swamp year. Both Aditi and I often think of you and tell other people about you, you know. That you had a year where you didn't write. I mean, we had no idea. And Clement was the same. His was a year of grieving and [pause] what was that swamp year?

> K: Well, I think it was partly like just complete, *what would you call it, like, meh, words,* [pause]. I think the whole idea that I couldn't do this that had come to dominate all my thoughts. *It was mostly self-inflicted.* I was also, as I now discover, clinically depressed. So, it was really kind of personal… [the interview breaks here].

Kay grieved the loss of her mother while she was finishing her master's. She had 'kind of managed' through that time, thinking she was fine, remarking that her family 'is very good at sweeping things under the carpet'. Grief and the imposter syndrome seem fused in overwhelming inertia:

> Basically, the sort of negativity of how I thought about myself, and I hadn't really processed things properly, missing my mom, it all culminated in this kind of inertia that I just could not escape. Ja, I mean, it was all those things, not just that I was stupid and would never amount to anything, and then also missing my mom, and not having you know, it was a lot of things. It was a low place emotionally. So it was a swampland in that period. So sometimes the group time [in the circle] was the only time I actually gave any thought to my PhD, because it was like front and centre, and the rest of the time I spent just, you know, the proverbial duck or swan or whatever, just trying to float, and still just kind of be normal. Anyway. That was the year in the swamp.

> L: It was amazing, because in that time you pitched up, you contributed, you read other people's work, you helped them design things, you know.

> K: Ja, all of that made me feel kind of worthwhile, I suppose. That I wasn't a complete waste of space. And I am a big believer in community, you know, so in many ways that was my community, even if I could not write the thesis, I could contribute.

Kay moves the focus on from the swampland to the group time of the circle. There are several moments in the interview when she repairs the pain with an explanation, a reflection on what the swampland was about, and how she found her way out of it. The very name 'swampland' is an act of repair. The sense of frozen inertia, just trying to stay afloat, seeming to be OK while no-one can see the panic underneath, is reminiscent of the way Clement experienced time described in Chapter 5 as feeling like a polar bear stuck in an iceberg, moving while not moving. The circle seems to mediate 'stuck' inner psychic time and external clock time.

Working with the interview I am struck by her analysis that the problems she experienced were 'self-inflicted', later modified with the mention that she was clinically depressed. Why would deep grief and an internalised sense of inadequacy around writing be self-inflicted like a wound? For Deleuze (2004), the wound is ongoing, it does not form a scar, but is lived out again and again in the quickening time of the event. Perhaps 'self-inflicted' speaks to the consequences of a neoliberal ethos. Support is on offer. If you can't take advantage of it for whatever reason, it's interpreted as a failure of the individual – 'kind of personal'. The pipeline notion of a container into which the student is packaged, where clock time is ticking, is in this moment a form of violence: profound grief, depression and alienation are not legitimate responses. The PhD has been commodified and the only valid concept of time is of time as money. With this framing, time is empty, to be filled in and ticked off as knowledge-making is caught up in a capitalist production and consumption cycle. To feel outside of these frameworks, and own the feelings, can be accompanied by a sense of shame, as in her saying that her problems were self-inflicted.

Kay also shares her frustrations with being stuck with the 'developing world' segment of knowledge, a paint by numbers exercise that would only ever be seen in terms of the frameworks of the global north. Her descriptions of the politics as in this description of a previous job as 'one of four research associates, one each in the countries, so South Africa, Brazil and China, and one in the UK, it seemed like our major role was to gather the data!' are wry and make me laugh with her in solidarity. The feelings of anger, amusement and shame provide openings for ongoing conversations, for revising, reworking, validating. Perhaps these feelings also resonate with my experience of losing a parent while completing a master's degree. Reading her words after the interview puts me in touch with that bruise and my own complicated feelings that I managed to finish my own master's degree at all, and what was betrayed in the process.

'A time to listen' in a 'situation that is evolving': Siwela

The interview with Siwela also starts 'in the middle' as we catch up on our lives and discuss his interest in further studies in the US. Like Kay, Siwela's brief time in the circle while he was on sabbatical in Cape Town is remembered as a time when he was able to be single-minded about his PhD. In my interaction with Siwela in the interview, he is working out how to describe his writing practices as fluid and itinerant, an aspect of his nomadic life at the time. As he says in the interview: '...so it was to find that kind of, like writing there becomes, you try to fit it in within a situation that is evolving'. In the written piece, he creates an image of the ecology of his writing life at that time from a position in the present:

> I would have to depict the coffee shops, formal and informal spaces that were a part of the writing, my mobility between Johannesburg, Pretoria, Cape Town and back to Pretoria. My residences frequently changed and I moved between these three big cities throughout the PhD. In hindsight, I write and think best when I am in 'discontinuous' conditions rather than being permanently located within one physical space. I can hardly spend my usual 10 or more hours of working per day in one office. This itinerant habit was crystallised during the PhD. The basic facilities such as, table, internet, power, good coffee seem to suffice for my writing, among strangers, temporal spaces, conditions, and times.

He expands on this in the interview as he reflects on that time of flux, with writing integral to mobility:

> [...] but now I think I didn't realise while I was busy, at that moment my life, in a way, was changing a lot. In the sense that while I was finding a home, setting up a home, adjusting, moving around, also to get closer to

work, as well, and at the same time, being able to keep the writing going, and in a way make it maybe less strenuous by finding something like a coffee shop, but not only just less strenuous, but also just finding a place available, because you cannot really be finding the ideal traditional laboratories or labs or postgraduate centres where you are situated in one campus. So it was to find that kind of, like writing there becomes, you try to fit it in within a situation that is evolving.

I ask if the decision to be supervised at the University of Cape Town and to spend sabbatical time there added more unwelcome uncertainty at the time:

So [the decision to be supervised in Cape Town], was like saying, 'Oh I am making this big move', it was almost done without too much trepidation, but almost with a convenient, agency for convenience at that particular time.

This description seems to embody what is expressed by Casey ((1993) in Janz (2001: 395)) as 'One does not move *to* a dwelling, but *dwells by moving*'. Home does not pre-exist. The sense of dwelling-by-moving is most vividly evoked in the interview with Siwela, perhaps because of the open distance learning institution where he works, and the consequences of his choice to register at a university at the other end of the country. There is a feeling of openness and emergence in his reflections. His expression of an itinerant self challenges the way we can think about agency, not as identity, but as emergent. The 'agency for convenience' that Siwela speaks of is not about fixing a time or place; it is about becoming as an ongoing lived enactment, rather than about identity in any settled sense.

Given this 'evolving situation' the circle took on a particular meaning for him – the only place where he was solely focused on the experience of being a doctoral student. He describes the circle as 'the only sounding board at those moments when I was not working on anything else but writing the dissertation. It made me look forward to developmental writing that is not really focusing on the product but rather on the process'. What was most valuable about the circle seems to have been the talking and the listening, as he writes:

[...] because there was always adequate conversation from the introductions [to each other in the circle], to the talk around the text, that it made more impact than the comments written on paper. It therefore was a time to listen. I perhaps enjoyed the listening to people the most.

The importance of 'talk around text'[1] in the circle pedagogy is reinforced in the interview when I remember moments where circlers thought he was a member of the police, rather than studying literacy practices of police who have chosen to become postgraduates:

[thought you were a policeman] Ja, it was always, the thing is, now that I think about it, it has always meant that I always have to go back to explaining who am I, and what is my role in this kind of environment. And maybe it took a while to do that, when I was starting the PhD, and gradually I became better at it. And I think now I am even the best at it now.

Because we are both interested in literacy practices, he describes what was 'perhaps a different kind of pedagogy' that came with the circle:

[...] where writing comes from a position of not being taught by an expert, to a time where one is able to talk about their writing. And hear how people perceive what is written, and basically being able to worry less about correctness or appropriacy but rather, the two pages become the focus of attention. The circle would allow one to draw on any relevant material, background material that has to be brought to bear or has some impact on the current piece.

He returns to the practice of the circle's two pages, juxtaposing what the circle offers with writing for 'high stakes' when one is writing alone for the supervisors:

[...] but maybe taking it from a much more meaning-making [approach] step-by-step from the two pages, like you said, it would just be an extract for two pages. Because you could just take them from anywhere, I found that quite rich.

I am struck by the particular meanings the circle has for him. He had written that the circle is the one place where writing moves completely out of the hands of powerful others and is placed firmly in the hands of 'strangers'. Its value is in writing among strangers, rather than offering community, which was so important for Kay and for other circlers who came regularly. In describing his writing ecology, the facilities – 'internet, power, good coffee' – among peers who are strangers are foregrounded. Apart from his six months in the circle, he had no writing community in Gauteng Province where he worked. He doesn't refer to the circle as an alternative writing community though. Different kinds of community had been essential for his wellbeing. In the interview we talk about his church community, and how recently in some ways his fellowship with marathon runners has become more important. These communities offer what Anne Herrington and Marcia Curtis (2000) call 'sponsoring discourses', often found alongside secondary discourses (Gee, 1990) acquired beyond the home but outside the academy. These sponsoring discourses enable a platform for connection, continuity and agency to keep going. It is often religion that provides this supportive cocoon where students draw strength for dealing with challenges in alienating spaces (Bangeni & Pym, 2017). Faith in particular is integral to Siwela's journey, notably in taking those most challenging steps that are beyond one as an individual. 'I felt partly that I had to rely on faith when I did not know what else, what comes next' when there are things that are 'beyond one's abilities', materially, emotionally or spiritually.

Early in the interview as we transition from catching up with recent events to reflecting on the PhD writing experience, I ask how it was to revisit the thesis. He responds that it was 'a bit like sentimental, and a bit emotional, because I think maybe there was an affective dimensional to it, which maybe at the time I tried to ignore and all that'. The words chosen to describe the experience hold back from naming it for what it was. He recalls a talk that he had given at an event where recently graduated PhDs in the Academic Literacies field had been invited to reflect on their research journeys. I was also present. He says:

> S: I think you asked me something and I said *I think I am recovering from trauma.*

The transcript records the laughter of both of us after he says this. I go back and listen. It's not easy to put the laughter into words. It feels that I laugh nervously, Siwela laughs wryly. I pursue the trauma thought and ask whether he would like to email me his presentation for the Academic Literacies forum. He says, 'I don't remember, I just thought about it, casually, or hesitantly, not necessarily like going back to my old files to find where it is'. I encourage him to go back to it feeling that it might be 'sort of relevant in terms of time healing the trauma in some kind of way, or reopening the trauma now and thinking about it, I don't know, it might be quite interesting'. He responds:

> S Ja. *I suppose trauma is not the right word.* Maybe it is because English is not my first language, maybe that is why I am doing further studies. So maybe there should be other more pleasant words.

> L No, I think trauma might well be just the right word, I don't know [laughter, L and S]

> S: I am trying to take you away from that word.

It is me, not him, who doesn't want to let go of the word trauma, introducing the word 'healing', persisting so he says 'maybe it's not the right word', ascribing the confusion to a series of possible explanations: maybe it's because English isn't his first language, maybe there are more pleasant words. We are stuck in the deficit discourse here. But not really, because we are laughing. The talk about trauma is the punctum for me in coming back to the interview, reminding me of the discomfort of feeling that I had been too controlling as a supervisor, and perhaps this is a chance to acknowledge it and move on. When I come back to listen to the interview again, it is the laughter alongside the word trauma that is the punctum – that pricks me, that feels like 'the cast of the dice' as Barthes (1981: 27) puts it.

'Sort of on my side, with strings' in 'The CEO of my project': Tia

The interview starts in the middle in a different way with Tia. There is some personal catching up, but the weight of words is in the lengthy ethical and theoretical justification from me. Tia has published on the ethics of her PhD, we have had discussions about the pedagogy of the circle, and she has given me robust feedback in the circle on my two pages from this manuscript about the writers' circle. She has also been a research assistant on a project I was involved with.

For her, the circle also offered something different within the tangle of practice of her writing ecology. Like Siwela, it was not her primary community or a safe space. In her written piece, Tia draws what she calls an 'organagram' listing the different elements of her PhD support structure. In a similar inversion to the waste picker who she positioned as her CEO, she uses the objectivity of an organogram to classify the different forms of emotional support she had while writing her thesis. The organogram is introduced by an explanation of how she categorised everything, making herself 'CEO of my project'. She turns the usual narrative about a PhD being a struggle on its head, reinserting it into a business efficiency model. She takes ownership of the words 'used and abused this to the max' and 'exploited' the PhD because 'everyone knows it's a struggle'. She laughs at herself recognising that the email to the course administrator that I refer to below is 'quite funny' in retrospect. The humour continues as she interrupts herself while writing to pretend to 'look up' the meaning of ecology to make sense of my email request in preparation for the interview:

> I have just read it [an email sent to the administrator in Sociology asking for feedback on the PhD process] and a few things strike me as quite funny, but also quite telling about how I approached the PhD emotionally and its ecology. Hold on. Going to look up what ecology means....ok. organisms and their relationship to the surroundings. I think what I am about to describe fits.

> Firstly, I categorise everything. Even in the email, I have put things in a numbered list. This is a small thing but an indication of how I approached the PhD emotionally. Although I was tackling a very sensitive subject, in terms of the project as a whole, I was pretty cold and ruthless! I compartmentalised everything and made myself CEO of the project. If I had to draw my relationship to the other things, people and spaces that got me through, it would undoubtedly be an organogram. See how I say how my supervisor is easy to manage – I treated him like he was part of my work team or an employee! Everyone had a specific function and *I used and abused this to the max*. One of the nice things about doing a PhD is everyone knows it is a struggle so you can use this to exploit others because they on some level feel a bit sorry for you! *Maybe exploit is the wrong word*. But you can certainly draw on the good will of others and use the PhD story as leverage.

In describing the 'nice things' about doing a PhD, Tia writes that because we all know it's a struggle, you can 'use this to exploit others because they on some level feel a bit sorry for you! Maybe exploit is the wrong word. But you can certainly draw on the good will of others'. The word she revises and checks is 'exploit'. Tia is creating her own constellation, orchestrating time, people, resources to her ends. For the most part, it works. The circle is the one part that is 'unpredictable' and does not involve unconditional support. Perhaps the instability of the circle offers a vital form of volatility in her project. In her written piece, she says 'The circle juxtaposes with the other groups that make up my team. It is an uncertain space where support is to some extent conditional, whereas in the other columns, support is unconditional because these relationships have longer and stronger roots'.

This is how the circle is described in the organogram she had drawn up:

- People I don't know well at all.
- People who don't necessarily know or understand me or my work.
- People who I potentially find very aggravating.
- A space to test run everything no matter how crap it is.
- A place that is full of surprises, ideas, inspiration, creativity.
- A place to practice how to talk to people, how to talk about research.
- Sort of on my side but at a distance and with strings.

She summarises the difference between her core support people and what was on offer through the circle: 'They [core support] were my bread and butter whereas circle was like a filling, except you are not quite sure if you will like it or not!'.

In the interview she elaborated on some of the aggravations, and also the way the circle offered a 'space to test run'.

> So you just, it [test running ideas] happened lots of times. I felt really bad because, you know, you got your name written on the PhD, but it is such a collective effort. And there are so many little things people do and say, you know, little suggestions.

Preceding this research inquiry, over the years Tia and I have had an ongoing conversation about the function and value of the writers' circle. Tia has always wanted to promote the writer circle, experiencing, I think, some frustration with my refusal to put it forward as a solution or a valuable resource. Coincidentally, while writing about the punctum in this engagement and analysis of interviews, I read an email she had sent me asking whether she could bring a new colleague to the circle. I had kept the email in case evidence for the impact of the circle was needed at some stage. There were attachments to the email, including a paper about her PhD methodology which had been accepted for the journal *Qualitative Enquiry*, with this explanation. Her concern with 'abusing' the space is expressed here too:

> I know you never pay any mind to tracking the impact that the circle has. But in the event that you ever need to demonstrate the value of the circle (Maybe you embroiled in a hidden battle to justify the tea trolley) and for your own interest, I have attached two things that are a direct result of using (abusing?!) the space.

In the interview, I pick up on our ongoing conversation about her relationship to the circle. Seeking her opinion, I share a comment from a colleague, who felt that writers' circles only made sense in well-resourced institutions. Tia has a different view:

> I see it as something that is one among many things, you may or may not have. I mean, so OK, if you didn't have access to conferences you wouldn't be coming in [to the circle] and presenting a dry run of your conference presentation, so you wouldn't have that. But I think the best thing was the two pages thing. That it is just whatever you got, you print it off, you bring it in, and it, you know. And that is what you are working with. And yea, everyone's level of supervision or quality of supervision varies. You can be at the most well-resourced institution, and your supervisor is an absolute shocker.

In returning to the written piece the punctum for me in this event is in 'abused to the max', revised to 'maybe exploit is the wrong word'. It hooks me as a rich point because like Siwela and Kay, the phrase involves an uncertainty about language, a testing out of the psychological and moral dimensions of doctoral studies, a dilemma expressed in feeling 'bad' but still making use of the expertise in the circle. Tia's uneasiness about using resources is a trouble spot, an open crack that she revisits again and again. She gave back to the circle richly, offering quality feedback, helping people who were stuck by writing alongside them outside of the circle, sharing her knowledge from NVivo coding workshops, generally bringing quality and commitment to all the workings of the circle. In the interview she talked more about her academic identity and relationship to privilege in higher education and how that played out in her PhD. As an international student from the UK, people assume she is privileged. She explains how 'strange it was coming from the UK, being working class, first in family to go to university, a child who was on free school meals, teenage mom, all of that' to immediately on arrival in South Africa 'being very very privileged, that was something I didn't expect [...] you have to note that, but you can't just be, "Well no, back home I am really poor", it is like no one gives a shit [laughs]'. The trouble with privilege and access to resources is kept open and revisited.

For all three of the interactions explored above, there is something else unfolding beyond the pretext, the focus on the circle in context. There is a sense of an ongoing upwelling as the past and the future interact in a small crack, a fountain that continues to bubble up, going over old ground, but subtly transforming it in the becoming of the present. This moment involves reflexivity, uncertainty, complicity and laughter that 'sees itself' (Verran, 1999, as described in Chapter 4) – an open-ended opportunity for us all to re-work past and future, to transform. Returning to Lapping's (2017: 917) research introduced in Chapter 5, these moments of submersive time can be read as a 'build-up of massed potential connections' where the numbing and often humiliating effects of duration are overturned, however briefly, by affective possibilities. If I had approached these interviews with the tools of conventional qualitative analysis, these moments would have seemed peripheral, superficial – phatic rather than substantial.

The intersecting experiences of Kay, Siwela, Tia with me have brought us together for this chapter. I am interested in what the circle means to the three ex-circlers as they look back, but as Siwela said, 'you are taking me back in time. But you will see, it will be back into the future, to use some science fiction writing'. He doesn't only want to be seen as my PhD student, way back then where the word 'trauma' resides. He is reaching forward, beyond his PhD to share another part of himself – a self that is involved in collaborations with other universities beyond South Africa. Past and future bleed into each other offering signs for a different reading of doctoral writing in the context of what Chihota (2007) calls 'the postgraduate condition': like the human condition, it is necessarily complex and paradoxical: there are no straight lines or pipelines.

'You will see, it will be back to the future': Time and Punctuation

The idea of punctuation offers us a way of reading the interactions in this chapter through several gaps, or cracks. The cracks that appear between speaking and transcribing, between interaction and analysis, are endlessly open to revision and transformation. In a similar way, we can read the circle as punctuation in the flow of each person's writing life. For each person, it offered a different rhythm and resonance, 'nice regular stitches', a 'place with strings' or a place for listening. This elaborates on the argument in Chapter 1, that the circle is not a safe space in any uncomplicated way.

In rendering embodied speech as a transcript, and then rendering it further in academic discourse, the written word cannot catch up with, or represent, the affect that saturates the present. In the gap between the research artefacts (written pieces and interviews) and my analysis, there is a punctum – a sharp moment where the three ex-circlers are struggling for words, and where these words pierce me. For Kay, it is when she is describing the swampland of stuckness, when she had been in an inert, frozen space of grieving. Her struggle was 'mostly self-inflicted. I was also, as I now discover, clinically depressed. It was kind of personal'. The word that shoots out between us most strongly is 'self-inflicted'. This is preceded by an overt struggle for expression, 'what do you call it, meh, words' and a long pause.

In the interview with Siwela, it is the word trauma that we both struggle over. He introduces it in a light way, 'casually or hesitantly', saying, 'I am trying to take you away from that word' but I seem interested in hanging on to it. In the face of the trauma and struggle narratives about the difficulties of the PhD journey, Tia tries to turn it on its head, saying that you can use this story of suffering as common knowledge ('everyone knows') and that you 'can use this to exploit others – maybe exploit is the wrong word. But you can certainly draw on the good will of others'. I see these words as a glide, or stumble, between past and future, all pointing to the difficulty with how to communicate the complexity of the post-graduate condition and how that unfolds in the experience of doctoral writing. In each case, a word or phrase is erased, weighed, found wanting in the telling. There is awkwardness, pausing, a shift in tone, with humour never far away. It is impossible to render or punctuate these parts of the interviews without risking something. Barthes writes about the punctum as involving 'an accident' and 'a cast of the dice': it is risky. If we read the punctum as affect, it is as Massumi (2015: xi) says, political, in that it points to an edge where we can manoeuvre 'where we might be able to go and what we might be able to do' in any given situation. Our agency in the moment 'corresponds to how much of an experiential depth we can access towards a next step'. This experiential depth is relational, felt by both the ex-circlers and by me. The interfaces created by the interview don't constitute a hard line that can be drawn round an event sealing it in the past: they are thick with the potentials of surface tension.

The chapter ends with a reflection from the ethics process for these interviews. Ethics processes are highly institutionalised and routinised. But they are also opportunities to keep meaning open. When Siwela read this description during our interaction for the ethics process, he said his work was more 'like a kaleidoscope. I wake up thinking about one thing but by the time I sleep I have traversed many areas'. In another comment he wrote 'My work was and is about crossings and becoming (in Faith)'. He seemed to be resisting closure, resisting my narrative which seeks causes and purposes, resisting my narrow interpretation of his research interests, based on my knowledge of him as supervisor. The ethics process reminds us that what looks like an ending is also a pause.

Note

(1) 'Talk around text' is a way of doing ethnographic research to explore literacy practices. The term is from Theresa Lillis' (2008) exploration of different levels of doing ethnographic research on writing and social practice. This is a text we both knew well in our relationship as student and supervisor.

7 'I remember a few rogue popcorns': Teaching for the Trace

with Clement Chihota and Aditi Hunma

> *Hungry translation can be seen as a non-stop striving for ethical retelling [...] despite the challenges of walking together on an uneven terrain, and despite an understanding that each retelling will be incomplete and imperfect.*

> Richa Nagar (2023: 5) Refusals, radical vulnerability, and hungry translations – A conversation with Richa Nagar. *Fennia-International Journal of Geography*

This co-written chapter moves further beyond the circle event, venturing out in time and space to engage the three facilitators who have held the space since its inception. It involves a plunge into the trace archive to retrieve sights and sounds and thoughts that have stayed with us in memory. Using Denis Hirson's (2004) repetitive opening 'I remember', we write separately and together to arrive at an assemblage of the circle from the perspective of the teachers who have held the space. Our memories of the circle create a vivid sketch of the sights and sounds of the trace. It is a form of 'hungry translation' (Nagar, 2019) – a journey of travelling together without guarantees. But the feeling of nostalgia that emerges asks more questions.

Aditi's words shape this chapter as she recalls memories from the circle:

> I remember that the only trace we left after the two hours together would be a few rogue popcorns that had flown in the air and settled lightly between the sheets of research.

Popcorn is cheap. One of us would go down to the cafe and buy a plastic bag of popcorn at the kiosk. Most of the time that was all we had on the table to go with the tea and coffee. There was always more than enough. The rogue popcorns that Aditi mentions are telling as there are signs everywhere instructing us not to take food into lecture theatres. But this isn't a lecture theatre. It's the 5th Floor Meeting Room. We hope to turn the room on its head by making it hospitable. Rogue popcorn is unruly. It resists being swept up neatly and somehow there are always left-over traces that have evaded our attempts to tidy up. They are the tell-tale residue of the writingwork that took place the day before. The sheets of research that Aditi refers to are either taken home after the circle, or loosely gathered in the yellow folders described in Chapter 2. They are approximations towards the expensive pages that might manifest in the formal archive as theses, peer reviewed articles and books. The unruly popcorn will eventually decay, perhaps leaving a tell-tale stain or a hard kernel like a stone in a shoe.

We – Clement, Aditi and I – bring together our memories of the circle as the three facilitators since the circle began. We immerse ourselves in the trace archive to expand the notion of the archive as 'the set of all events that can be recalled across time and space' (Bowker, 2010: 212). Through these sights and sounds, we challenge the imaginary of the sedimented written forms of the formal archive as we embrace what Richa Nagar (2019) calls radical vulnerability. This vulnerability rests on reluctance to continue to oil the wheels of the old knowledge machine that churns out knowledge *as if nothing had been left out*. Nagar's work is radical and engaged over time, emerging from highly collaborative grassroots activism, years of working with marginalised communities in India. This book, and particularly this chapter, cannot hope to claim the politics that her years of engagement inspire. I like to think that there are some similarities though. For Richa Nagar, radical vulnerability is a necessary part of hungry translations, the term she uses to describe their collaborative approach to knowledge-making. This approach comes out of 'intense relationality and co-ownership of dreams among those who occupy different locations in predominant epistemic hierarchies' (2019: 30). Hungry translations emerge outside of conventional protocols for inquiry. They are part of shared journeys that are obliquely positioned to upset the contours of dominant knowledge paradigms:

> In resisting formulaic modes of defining citational architectures or methodological approaches, and in radically reimagining the temporalities and meanings of knowledge-making partnerships, these translations demand a collectively embraced radical vulnerability in which the individual ego must surrender to a politics of co-traveling and co-authorship that involves difficult refusals. (2019: 33)

She calls her approach to inquiry a form of 'agitation' (Nagar & Selmeczi, 2019: 9) that involves 'the work of engaging in an ongoing relation between self and other despite the unevenness of the terrain in which such translations take place' (Nagar *et al.*, 2023: 6). This work is animated by 'an unshakeable belief in the creativity that emerges from a shared journey – one in which the risks and dangers are frequently accompanied by the joys and promises of long-lasting bonds, community, and struggles for justice (Nagar *et al.*, 2023: 2).

An important element in hungry translations is the refusal – moments of resistance, solidarity, confusion, uncertainty – that show up the complexity of power, but also show up forms of epistemic violence. Our choices to resist formulaic, normative ways of doing things permeate this chapter.

We explore our knowledge-making partnership as facilitators as we co-travel in this chapter. This journey together is risky as we enter this process of re-telling as a relationship: 'The labour and poetics of forging togetherness across difference [...] can only realise their transformative potential as politics without guarantees' (Nagar & Shirazi, 2019: 242). Co-travelling smudges the I – the subjectivity that has both compelled and hobbled me in the writing of this book – towards a we, that lovely sense of the collective energy of doing something different together. In this way our research process for this chapter mimics the most productive aspects of the circle. In Chapter 1, the introduction to the writers' circle space, the re-creation of one of the more challenging circles described how our talk at the end of the circle 'brings out the best in us' with constructive, ethical critique. In that story, our talking together in the circle and the way Elizabeth mimicked our different stances 'acting out disbelief, sorrow, relief, scepticism and scholarly concern in turn' leaves us at a point where we can laugh and experience a kind of academic bliss that is not easy to find. But there are also hesitations, resistance and silences that come into this chapter, in our recall of key moments and insights in the circle, and in reflection after working together.

There are threads that hold us three facilitators together loosely, though Clement and Aditi have never met in person (but they have heard about each other from colleagues who are also mutual friends). We have all worked in research writing development and share a deep interest in the dynamics and politics of writer voice. There is another kind of thread that I feel again in reading our entries and conversations in working on this chapter: a southern African affinity, sense of humour and seriousness in the postcolonial quirkiness of our situations. Clement has since made a new path for himself as a lecturer in Social Work at universities in New Zealand and then Australia. At the time of our working together, he wrote a short bio noting that the circle 'felt like "alternative" leftist spaces that advanced equity, social justice and empowerment within the academy'. Aditi's master's and PhD had both looked at the writing struggles and accommodations of Mauritian and International students at the University of Cape Town.

When we started to work together on this chapter, Clement was in Melbourne and, while both Aditi and I were in Cape Town, we were in deep lockdown, physically separated by the pandemic and unable to meet. Aditi was running the circle online. As an entry point into a conversation, we created a shareable document in Google Drive where each of us separately wrote a series of statements in which we recalled experiences of facilitating the circle. We drew on the formulaic openings used by Denis Hirson (2004) in 'I remember King Kong (the boxer)'. Hirson begins each stanza with the words, 'I remember...', the openings acting as a hook for a memory of growing up in apartheid South Africa in the 1950s and 60s.

Hirson's sentences segue from highly specific, seemingly banal memories such as 'I remember the sting of a wet tennis ball' (2004: 11) and 'I remember that a mouse bit a hole through my brown cardboard nursery school case' (2004: 18) to more freighted ones such as 'I remember that when my father came out of prison he grew his side-burns down to the earlobes to catch up with the times'[1] (2004: 130) and 'I remember my father at a friend's house talking in an urgent hush about Sharpeville,[2] and the peace and sunlight in the garden outside' (2004: 49). The naming of these traces creates a powerful sense of innocence but also of menace, capturing, sometimes even in the same sentence, the experience of growing up in a deeply distorted and dysfunctional society in which moments of normality are intercut with terror and trauma. Perhaps this way of inaugurating the sentence with 'I remember' can help to access the often-hidden sides to the postgraduate experience such as the stuckness and clogged misery, among moments of growing awareness, shared connections and generally feeling alive and worthwhile.

Our writing and talking took place over several months with stops and starts. Writing brought us together, teacups in hand, to listen and grow. The dislocations and losses that each one of us had experienced during lockdown were slowly brought to our discussion and writing as we reconnected and reached out to one another. We wrote our initial statements beginning with 'I remember' in separate documents and then merged them on Google Docs, keeping the authors distinct. Then we commented on each other's entries, using the comments function in Google Docs. In working with what we wrote, we are interested in how we remember the circle. What are the sights and sounds we recall? What is it like to teach for the trace? How might we share this experience with others? What are the limits and possibilities in this process of writing and thinking together as we devise a way of co-travelling during the writing of this chapter?

In recreating our interactions below, our voices are initially separated out and named. Then towards the end of the chapter I no longer identify who is speaking and the voices of us three facilitators merge. In not attributing 'I remember' written memories to speakers, perhaps it is possible to glimpse the 'shared city' of memory as described by Hirson in the postscript to 'I remember King Kong (the boxer)'. He writes that 'By the time one has gone through a few hundred sentences beginning "I remember", the "I" might have dissolved in the remembering. Memory then becomes a potentially more selfless place, a shared city that can be seen with greater clarity than when one actually lived there' (2004: 135).

In our shared Google Docs folder there are two forms of comment. The first involves comments in the margins. We looked at these marginalia to find the places in the text that thickened and quickened, where there seemed to be most interest from all three of us. The second form of comment evolved in one of our later meetings where we ended up writing synchronously in layers over each other's 'I remember' written memories, using different coloured fonts that do not show up in the rendition in this chapter. So in the extract from the Google Doc below, Clement comments on Aditi's memory in the margins, and later, he comments underneath her text, 'We are juvenile delinquents...', as an extension of it. My synchronous comments begin 'I'm wondering...'.

Aditi Hunma

I remember how every Thursday at 3pm, a sober consultation room in the Writing Centre would become animated by a bunch of circlers and their two pages. We were in Hlanganani building then. And the staff lurking outside the four walls of that room would often ask me why we were laughing so much. They were shy to join in but in awe about the festive mood that overtook our Thursday afternoons. We were juvenile delinquents laughing at/about things that noone, including us, fully understood.

I'm wondering about your word lurking - did we create envy, did some feel excluded, were they wanting to join in or to 'report' us for being unruly.

I remember we often said to ourselves, 'What happens in Vegas, stays in Vegas!' Why did we say that? I will have to feign not to remember... But, was 'Vegas' a random location? Or was there an underlying sense that we came here to gamble, to experiment, to explore freely within an alternative space that permitted/licenced such experimentation?

I remember that the only trace we left after the two hours together would be a few rogue popcorns that had flown in the air and settled lightly between the sheets of research. Oh and also the lipstick on cups of tea that had served their guests more than once. Yes we were mostly women in the group for some strange reason.

> **Anonymous**
> 6 Dec 2019
>
> The two pagers fascinate me. what was their role/effect? Where they a form of currency - to enable exchanges between members? Did they serve to 'kick start' more extensive writing processes? Where they confidence building props?
>
> **Aditi Hunma**
> 16 Jul 2020
>
> Why did I use the word 'animated' here? Was it the space that animated the participants, or the participants that
> Show more

The three different forms of interaction are signposted in the rest of this text in the following ways:

- **Memories of the circle, beginning with** *I remember* ...: the three of us writing independently of one another: *I remember* how ...
- **Synchronous writing** as an overlay on our original entries: *I'm wondering about* ...
- **Comments in the margins**, written separately: The two pages fascinate me...
- [A], [C] and [L] denote who was writing. Towards the end of the chapter, these are no longer used.

The reader is invited to feel the rhythm of the 'I remember' opening as a sort of a chant, perhaps in the spirit of Hirson's shared city. The expectation of 'a smooth read' (Turner, 2018: 231) is not met here. The reading experience may feel a little like trying to gather unruly popcorn.

I remember ...

I remember the way the sink in the 5th floor meeting room in Hoerikwaggo gurgled for no apparent reason, rather like a tummy rumbling. We always laughed. It was a comment on our seriousness. [L] *To play with the word gurgle, strangle, throttle, full throttle, throat, deep throat, voice.* [L]

I remember not knowing why people came once and never again [L]. *Or why some continued to come back again and again. [C]*

I remember having to bite my tongue during some difficult encounters [L]. *Tongue biting was not new in this space – a topic or a text could lead the interaction in any unknown direction – and biting the tongue felt like applying some kind of weak brake that would obviously not stop the discursive momentum. [C] Tongue biting and gurgling – our words are so embodied. Love the idea of a weak brake, the spilling over would still be felt in some way. Affect carries the discursive momentum...[L]*

I remember when Terry and Albie approached reproduction and reproductive rights from such different angles, and they laughed and shook hands. [L]

There are comments in the margin from both Clement and Aditi next to my recall of the circle with two participants in the circle, Terry and Albie, debating reproductive rights:

```
Circles as spaces of rehearsal in two senses.
Members test out their ideas in this safe space
before taking them to more threatening/ high stakes
audiences. At another level, 'wild' theories/ideas
are tested out before being integrated into formal
academic texts. In this case, appear to have engaged
in some 'intellectual sparring'. [C]
```

```
Very true! A beautiful imagery. There was also an
undercurrent to the discussion. One of the debaters
identifies as queer/non-binary, and the other ini-
tially appeared opposed to such 'transgressions'. I
was expecting the worst – an explosion of sorts.
But, Albie was very respectful and asked questions
about Terry's gender identity. The questions were
far from neutral though, but the laughter at the
end just shows at some point they both agreed to
call it quits. [A]
```

We move between highly specific memories, many that involve vulnerability, and more general reflection and theorising about what is going on. This speaks to Barad's (2012: 207) mode of theorising as being in touch, attuned to the 'world's patternings and murmurings'.

On Not Putting your Suitcase on the Ground

One of Clement's memories introduces the idea that we are intellectual nomads. Both Aditi and I comment on this:

I remember realising that academia was akin to the proverbial Rome – that it had numerous roads leading to it. For, how was it that the sciences and humanities appeared to converge around certain values – and epistemologies? How did it happen that students from so-called 'non-cognate' disciplines spoke the same language, and incisively critiqued each other's work? Could it be that in the writer circles, we all became intellectual nomads – intolerant of walls and disciplinary boundaries – and we inhabited that liminal zone where disciplines merge and forget their class – and tribal – divisions? [C]

```
Powerful!! I guess the circle was avant-garde in
this. Because presently, in wider academic spaces,
we notice some academics tiptoeing into each oth-
er's territories /disciplines. The idea of nomad-ry
is so apt, for how can one be a seeker of knowledge
if one has already put one's suitcase on the
ground? [A]
```

```
Lovely. They are totally different ways of being.
With a suitcase, one is there to stake out a terri-
tory? [L]
```

We have gone from disciplines to nomads to asking whether it is possible to be a knowledge-seeker if one has 'already put one's suitcase on the ground'. We see the circle as a space for traversing between disciplines. Disciplines are typical spaces for the operation of Derrida's (1996) jussive archive with its bundles for organising memory that wax and wane to hold what come to be seen as authoritative versions of knowledge. In its jussive function, the archive operates through leaving things out so the product comes to seem natural and inevitable. It acts in a way that is 'invisibly exclusionary' (Bowker, 2005: 14) as it seems to set the limits of what it is possible to think or do or say. Once you are inside a silo it becomes impossible to imagine another way of thinking or being. That silo becomes totalising. But there are ways to break these down in a politics from below. In his synchronous comments made live while we were reading the 'I remember' memories, Clement introduces the idea in the synchronous comments that we are like 'juvenile delinquents'.

Juvenile Delinquents

I remember how every Thursday at 3pm, a sober consultation room would become animated by a bunch of circlers and their two pages. We were in Hlanganani building then. And the staff lurking outside the four walls of that room would often ask me why we were laughing so much. They were shy to join in but in awe about the festive mood that overtook our Thursday afternoons. [A] *We were juvenile delinquents laughing at/about things that no-one, including us, fully understood.[C]*

```
I'm wondering about your word lurking – did we create
envy, did some feel excluded, were 'they' wanting to
join in or to 'report' us for being unruly. [L]
```

On a few occasions, we were asked to stop bringing popcorn to the space because of the mess it created. It seemed to show us up as rogues too. We decided henceforth to leave no trace of our 'delinquency' upon leaving the space. The ritual reminded me of 'AfrikaBurn' – where collective minds created something together, then disappeared without leaving behind any sign. The creative process and collaboration took precedence over what was created and who owned it – hence the deliberate effacing at the end. [A]

I *remember* the struggles of trying to make decisions during the #RhodesMustFall shutdown. Should we meet? If so, where? The Baxter, Aditi's flat, CoCoWahWah, the tea house next door? Every space seemed to be loaded, to include some and exclude others [L]. *The writer circle needed to occur in a neutral space – accessible and comfortable to all. It could not thrive in a space strongly stamped by any single character, personality or culture. It was the quintessential 'confluence'. [A]*

I *remember* we often said to ourselves, 'What happens in Vegas, stays in Vegas!' Why did we say that? I will have to feign not to remember… [A]. *But, was 'Vegas' a random location? Or was there an underlying sense that we came here to gamble, to experiment, to explore freely within an alternative space that permitted/licenced such experimentation? [C]*

I *remember* the circles as always fraught with uncertainty. Participants were not obligated to attend, and full circles, week after week, would always surprise. More uncertainty came from not knowing what participants from various disciplines or at different stages of their research/writing journeys would bring to the table. Ironically, this uncertainty made each writer circle feel almost like a new beginning. There would be a core of participants who attended the circles every week, often mixed with new faces that always managed to shift the group dynamic and ecology (to be continued). [C]

I *remember* how each time circlers introduced themselves or their research, it sounded similar but *differant* (displaced in time). I had to bring in Derrida, like the many scholars that we circlers had intellectual crushes on. [A]

I *remember* feeling I was a part of this group – not in the proprietary sense of owning or running the group process – but more in the sense of being owned and shaped by it. Here, the distinction between instructor and learner was irrelevant – and the claim to even be a 'facilitator' was problematic. We simply sat together like fellow travellers journeying towards an unknown destination. Explorers *feeling our way forward* together. Sharing that process equally with none of us knowing exactly where it would lead. Perhaps my only distinction was that I had travelled with other groups before – but not arrived at this elusive destination. In the circles, we allowed our conversations to flow – and any member could shape the direction.... Now, if *that* is 'facilitation', then so is the role of the person who initiates an idle conversation among strangers trying to kill time while waiting in a queue....[C]

```
I feel the same. Yesterday though, one of the members
urged me to cut the discussion on 'What is knowledge?'
so that we could get to her writing. I usually let it
stay organic, but yesterday, I succumbed to her
request because we were a bit pressed for time. [A]
```

It's not unusual for our recollections to involve descriptions of 'this far, no further' moments like this. A participant in Aditi's online circle got irritated with the organic discussion on what is knowledge and Aditi 'succumbed' to the request to move on to the main focus of the circle. These are moments of refusal, in which we choose not to oil the wheels of normative expectation and instead resist 'formulaic modes' (Nagar, 2019: 33). That is what Aditi does by holding back on facilitation in the interests of a meta-discussion about the politics of knowledge. These tilting points come to light in the politics of co-travelling for both participants in the circle and for us as facilitators. There are our refusals in our style of facilitation or in how this chapter comes together, but there are also the refusals of students, as they made their own way.

Refusals

Two of us remember Jo's green book that she brought to the circle. Every now and again Jo would take it out during a circle and write down a grammar rule.

I remember Jo's Green Book with all the rules, hints, tips. In her discipline you are not allowed to say 'According to...' She wanted more than the soft discursive space the circle offered.

I remember Jo's green book that could neatly have fit on the grammarian's altar.

We enjoyed the Green Book and teased Jo gently about it. As facilitators, we resisted being didactic about sentence-level grammatical structures and some conventions and styles, particularly those that varied across academic communities, such as whether it is OK to over-use 'according to' or to start a sentence with 'but'. But Jo wanted more certainties and tried to elicit them from us. As Jo was a new supervisor, being explicit about the conventions would have been reassuring for her. So she developed her own practice of jotting down 'rules'.

The ethics process also offers opportunities for resistance for circlers. When I shared Chapter 4 on laughter with students for ethical clearance, Elena responded with a thoughtful reflection on the way the circle worked, including the observation that 'I think people who elect to attend the Thursday Circle are people who can sit with their vulnerability'. In our ethics process for this chapter, I shared a section with a student where I discuss a moment of doubt and vulnerability around whether I had understood his work. The student gave us feedback that in the circle, and in our recall of moments in the circle, we had overlooked the most important part of the research, and there was 'no value' in including our memories of the project in this book. He was not willing to give consent. One person's sense of vulnerability is another's sense of betrayal.

We remember Elizabeth's cartoon of the blind men and the elephant that she wanted to put on the first page of her phenomenological study of caring for patients with cancer, discussed in Chapter 3.

> *I remember* Elizabeth's elephant that never made it on page 1 of her thesis introduction. *I really love this moment in our collective memories. Just saw an email from her. I have to restrain myself so I don't run away with lines of flight that follow her — a beautiful person with healing laughter, she shed her name, she moved between research groups trying to get a foothold, to belong, she followed her supervisor to a city in the north (we gave her advice in the circle about how to dress while there!!) ...the elephant was a boundary object that she tried to bring in to make her work fresh and engaging. The group gently, I think, turned her away. Or did she end up using it?*

> *I remember* Vere's notebook and the shorthand script as she got more interested in the circle and its dynamics than in her research on social justice and identity. *Vere finding a new line of flight? Needing to depart from the set pathway into the discovery zone?*

For us three facilitators, throughout the written memories and our comments on them, our descriptions suggest our vulnerability in phrases like 'staff lurking outside', 'juvenile delinquents that nobody, including ourselves, understood', 'gambling', 'fraught with uncertainty', 'intellectual crushes', 'awkwardly hilarious (oxymoron intended)', 'tongue-biting', 'gurgling' (babies? death throes?) and 'lipstick' as a transgressive solidarity sets in for us through this process of writing our memories, comments in the margins and synchronous writing. In both the circle and our remembering of it together, we seem to want to keep things open indefinitely.

I have focused mainly on the memories and comments where there was dense interaction, where ideas and memories were sparked. Some entries were followed by silence – perhaps because they were banal, obscure, or because they were unsettling. An example is my comment in the margin, framed as a question, about the impact of the facilitator's identity on how the group was constituted and whether the circle could be thought of as a safe space. I was struggling with how to write about subjectivity and identity in authoring this book and was hoping that this might be a forum where we would talk about this. But I had to puzzle it out for myself. We were not able/ready to go there to talk about the difficult intersections of class, race, gender and age in how the circle is constituted – not here anyway. It was more important to preserve solidarity.

The Unsettling Affect of *I remember*

When I step back to reflect on the writing method we have used to reflect on the circle in this chapter, a problem emerges. It taps into the paradoxical work of nostalgia, always making a tricky deal between past and present. There is nostalgia – a particular form of affect – for me in writing these memories; a nostalgia for the meaning and comradeship of decades of work, initially when South Africa was in a State of Emergency as the anti-apartheid struggle intensified in the late 1980s, entering retirement in what I think of as a state of emergence during the #MustFall protests. Writing with my old colleagues during the pandemic amplifies this feeling. But it is complex and difficult to analyse from the inside and to do justice to the ethical issues raised. Hirson's book was a best-seller in South Africa, striking a chord with a largely white, privileged readership. Reflecting later on the experience of writing this chapter, I read Erica Lombard's article (2016) on the work of nostalgia in Hirson's book. Lombard writes that Hirson's use of the 'I remember' form is 'at risk of endorsing a troubling amnesia and defending ongoing inequality' (2016: 6). Retrieving the quotidien in South Africa then, in the apartheid regime, and now, is complex. As Melissa Steyn (2012) notes, an 'ignorance contract' is still in place, protecting racialised power.

As far back as 1986, at the height of the struggle that resulted in the formal end of apartheid, Njabulo Ndebele tried to look ahead to imagine another country rooted in the 'ordinary day-to-day lives of people…to engage with a range of complex ethical issues [...] within which vistas of inner capacity are opened up' (1986: 156). The 'I remember' form gives us some glimpses of inner capacity but at the same time asks complex ethical questions as writing involves a sustained inquiry into the relation between self and other 'despite the unevenness of the terrain', as Nagar (2019) puts it. Jacob Dlamini's memoir, 'Native nostalgia' (2009), tries to retrieve the ordinary in black life under apartheid to challenge the stuck narratives of hero, victim and perpetrator[3] that still present in local writing. Dlamini (2009) explicitly takes up Ndebele's invitation, acknowledging how unsettling the work of nostalgia can be. He confronts a conundrum: What does it mean that black life under apartheid 'was not all gloom and doom and there was a lot of which black South Africans could be, and were, proud?' (2009: 13). Facing this conundrum is not an attempt to justify apartheid. This step away from the interaction around our memories of the circle takes me down a path that is difficult and unfinished, taking me back to the affect of shame explored in Chapter 4. It is a reminder of Probyn's (2005: 162) point that shame and writing often go together because, writing is 'interested', and implicated, as we are 'deeply embedded in contexts, politics and bodies' as we write the difficult stuff in a commitment to ongoing struggle for ethical re-telling.

More Poetics than Didactics

Richa Nagar (2019: 33) ends Hungry Translations with a hopeful pedagogy, a series of Acts and Scenes that constitute a curriculum for a form of activism that involves telling stories from the field to 'reimagine the temporalities and meanings of knowledge-making partnerships by surrendering to a politics of co-travelling and co-authorship, politics that are accompanied by a difficult refusal'. I am not going to end this chapter or this book with a set of pointers for how to facilitate a writers' circle on the southern tip of the continent. I don't want to translate this exploration of the circle as a space for thinking about writing and knowledge-making into a plan for pedagogical action. This is instead a deep ethnography of an engagement in which writing is crucial, but in unexpected ways. Writing is what brings students to the circle, and it is what brings the circle into being as new assemblages emerge, as in writing this book, which is only possible through the 'brave spaces' (Arao & Clemens, 2013) I have shared with others. My interest in resonance and rhythm in writing and how this might bring the life of the circle closer has more in common with poetics rather than with didactics. In seeking affective attunement to the relational through writing, there is no 'blueprint' (Gibbs, 2005), and neither are there guarantees. Embracing resonance and rhythm, this kind of writing finds and loses itself, as subjectivity is risked.

The re-tellings that take place in and beyond the circle are like hungry translations. They are never expert or complete, always happening for the first time, endlessly renewing. They traverse disciplines. We can't put our suitcases down for long. These epistemic energies hold for both the praxis of the circle and for the way the three of us began to explore together for this chapter. We explain, confess, unpack, laugh, as we work together. For me (Lucia) there is the experience of nostalgia, a homesickness and longing for the camaraderie of working with Clement and Aditi. This longing never escapes the broader contextual historical structures and discourses of world-making from a southern perspective. Through hungry translations new assemblages come into being, enriching the stock of memory practices. As Bowker (2005: 7) writes, 'Scientific texts are written not to record what actually happened in the laboratory, but to tell the story of an ideal past in which all the protocols were duly followed'. Here memories surface not as facts that corroborate the protocols but as shards – fragments that give a glimpse of what can be carried forward into the future.

I close this chapter with a series of glimpses, neither analysed nor attributed:

I remember those times during the protests, when the circlers sympathised with the cause, but also chose to reconvene in lesser known spaces. It felt like going underground together. One after another, the members buzzed in. They grabbed a cushion once we had run out of chairs. All women this time… It didn't just feel cozy, but as though we had rallied in the same spirit of sisterhood. Our discussions around texts those days could not escape the weight of history and sociopolitical dilemmas. We interwove all this with the comfort of tea and beautiful writing of course.

I remember the times when the circle carried on till 6:30 pm and no one wanted to go home. The momentum had built up so much that members could no longer contain their thoughts and conversations. They were oozing from everywhere. I remember sitting back and smiling.

I remember the times when circlers would start networking, exchanging cards, inviting each other to book launches, reading each other's work in other spaces.

I remember the times when circlers would make it mandatory for their friends to attend, saying, 'This is good for you!' That would sit so awkwardly with me.

I remember other times, when circlers would wish to form their own departmental circles. It was special to witness the decalque (I am really hoping this is an English word too) of this circle. At times, the focus of the new circles shifted from engagement to compliance. But it was all in good spirit.

I remember how circlers would sometimes feel apologetic about their writing before sharing it, while those giving feedback would sometimes feel inspired by the text they had just read. It was fascinating how the act of reading and writing these texts created mind-waves in the way that the circlers imagined each other and themselves in the academic spheres.

I remember once worrying that a sudden outburst of laughter – after one member had shared a research proposal that sounded almost incoherent (and which I compared to wrestling with a strange animal in the dark) – might have come across as laughing at (rather than *with* that particular member). I later realised that this statement sort of captured our process – wrestling with a strange entity in the dark and not exactly sure what we were wrestling with.

I remember Adam explaining to a newcomer how the circle functions, '*everyone gives and everyone gets*'.

Notes

(1) Baruch Hirson, Denis' father, was an historian who was imprisoned for nine years for his anti-apartheid activism. After he was released, he was banned and went into exile in the UK with his family.

(2) The Sharpeville Massacre on 30 March 1960 is widely seen as a watershed in South African history, a catalyst for both resistance and repression. There is a detailed account at https://www.sahistory.org.za/article/sharpeville-massacre-21-march-1960

(3) Both Jacob Dlamini (2009) and Melissa Steyn (2012) write in the aftermath of the Truth and Reconciliation Commission (TRC). This ground-breaking initiative put us in a better position to engage more honestly with the past, but amongst other omissions, it obscured the everyday life of black South Africans who were smothered in a discourse of victim and perpetrator. Both writers explicitly address this blind spot.

Conclusion: Knowledge-Making at the Water Point

> *A body in the process of learning is a body blurred by*
> *its own indeterminacy and by its openness to an elsewhere*
> *and to an otherwise.*
>
> Elizabeth Ellsworth (2005: 122) *Places of Learning*

In the final chapter I explore what this quest for the trace means for writing and knowledge-making. By foregrounding processual qualities of teaching and research while keeping the formal archive in my peripheral vision, I draw attention to writing as a smudge, as unfinished, watery, flowing. The smudge, like surface tension, is at the interface between trace and formal archives, between subjective and objective, what is inside and what's outside. As both pedagogy and as research, I hope that it can disrupt deficit views of students by offering glimpses of inner capacity along the way, by pausing the moments of transition and by embracing how layered time plays out in research writing. The idea of writing as a smudge has a place alongside more traditional identify and induct approaches to writing pedagogy. Together they may form hybrid assemblages that can move and shape-shift with the currents to think new futures for knowledge-making through writing.

The trace lives lightly in the circle, with a changing collective of postgraduate writers and their teachers. Each figure in this collective is at the water point, a place to gather, vex, inspire while on the way somewhere else. In writing this book, I have tried to stay with the trace while always keeping an eye on divine discourse with its weight and consequences.

With text-work in the university, we are expected to cover our traces in the quest for an objective representation of the world. I have approached writing obliquely in order to bring the traces into view, taking a step back from the writing of research products such as theses and journal articles to 'see the traces, tracks and footprints of what might have been and what could be' (Badenhorst *et al.*, 2021: 13). I have tried to foreground the process without assuming the dominant narrative about the process/product binary – that we journey from messy beginnings to arrive at an inevitable chiselled, expensive product that counts in the formal archive of the academy. The imaginary for this ideal product is objective, scientific, effaced, as described in the optics of the god view with its textual correlate, divine discourse.

The questions guiding this inquiry are not text-focused. Questions such as these have given shape to this text:

What kind of space is the writers' circle?

How can the scraps left in the yellow folders guide us to the trace archive?

What does laughter in the circle mean and do, and how might we research it?

How does time play out in teaching writing and in the circle and in research about the circle, long after having been a member of the circle?

How do facilitators remember the circle?

How can we use concepts as productive interference to immerse ourselves in the circle and what it means and does?

How might we inquire into a process so that it can help us to imagine research writing differently?

Together these questions have given a sense of the sights and sounds from the circle as a particular kind of radically open crucible for knowledge-making. Writing is central but it is also peripheral. It catapults us in multiple directions at the same time. The slightly out-of-focus vantage point on the writing life of the changing collective of the circle is enacted in the choice I made to explore the circle using methods that embrace writing as inquiry, as an expression of ethical relationality that is both critique and affirmation. I am conscious of writing on the edges of disciplines and methodologies, not aiming to reveal the social practices that *should* constitute the canon on how to approach the writing of research. Rather than replicating social practices through writing, I have tried to write both with and against the grain, sometimes skidding joyfully only to encounter a dark corner again very quickly.

I have travelled with surface tension as a form of inventive interference (Law & Urry, 2004: 397) at play at the interface between the trace and formal archives, between subjective and objective and in the productive tension between what is inside and what is outside the writer's thought in the world. I hope that this way of working can help to strengthen particular processual affects and realities while backgrounding others.

Writing as a Smudge

Surface tension as concept-in-motion has led me to the idea of writing as a smudge. I first read about learning as a smudge in Kamler and Thomson's *Helping Doctoral Students Write: Pedagogies for Supervision* (2006). The idea can be traced back to feminist teacher Elizabeth Ellsworth's *Places of Learning: Media, Architecture, Pedagogy* (2005).

Finding inspiration in Massumi's work in processual philosophy (2002) and psychotherapist Donald Winnicott's idea of transitional spaces (1989), for Elsworth the notion of the smudge is a breeching of the self, expressed in a transitional moment of becoming. The emphasis is not on knowledge *made*, as in the formal archive, but on knowledge-*making*.

In relation to writing, smudging the ink is part of an old material practice associated with fountain pens and blotting paper – a writing technology that is fast fading. A smudge is the consequence of a hand moving across ink that has not yet dried, or perhaps of uneven application of ink, an unsteady hand or spilt liquid (tears?). The unsteady hand, imperfect tool dipped in an inkwell, textured paper, remind us of the materiality of writing – a reality that has been submerged with the dominance of digital composing where it is easier to erase, to delete without leaving a visible trace, and to start again. It also reminds us of bodies with continuity of movement and sensation. The word smudge rhymes with nudge, both suggest agential movement towards a next, but the next is not fixed. The writer and the writing are always emergent. Any textual product is but a moment that punctuates the flow.

The concept of writing as a smudge is thus a skid, slippage between fixed and binary terms, like process and product, surface and depth, trace and formal archive, correct and incorrect. It is an approach to writing that emerges from surface tension. It is always productive, never closed down. It is always imperfect but somehow reaching for more than can neatly be captured on the page.

The idea of the smudge can offer insight into both the pedagogy of the circle and into the way in which I have approached it through writing as inquiry.

Teaching Research Writing

It has not been my aim in this book to offer guidance on how to run a writers' circle, as I am sure that there should be many different approaches, as suggested in Starke-Meyerring's (2014) typology of different ways of organising a writing group. Living with the Thursday circle and writing about it here is a portal to wider issues and concerns about the relationship between writing and knowledge-making. The pedagogy of the circle embraces the smudge, more interested in thought-in-movement than in the representation of knowledge.

The vulnerability that emerged as Aditi, Clement and I worked together in the process of writing Chapter 7, where we sometimes feel like juvenile delinquents who cannot put their suitcases on the ground, is a way of teaching without guarantees as we try to hold an unsteady equilibrium at the interface. Our process in writing this chapter together mirrors some of the dynamics of the circle, with laughter and seriousness interconnected, as affect plays out at the surface.

The interactions in the circle where people haven't signed up for a curriculum with a particular course in mind, means that the knowledge, in the sense of a destination, with assessment practices, rankings, conformity (or not), gets backgrounded. The pedagogy happens through choosing a next in the form of two pages that are in the hands of the postgraduate scholar and of people outside of your discipline.

Researching the Circle

The vulnerability of the circle pedagogy is echoed in my approach to research. The edgy space of the circle has been approached through a rhizomatic deep ethnography re-made from scraps left behind in the wake of the circle. Memory, the unexpected contacts that emerge from synchronicity, tailor-made images, as well as new inquiry in the form of workshops and interviews, have also been resources for this study.

I have not used one method in this exploration of surface tension at the interface, instead choosing the most apt approaches and forms to do justice to the ethical relationality of writing as inquiry. There is no blueprint for this way of writing and researching as it 'must be constantly invented anew in the face of the singular problems that arise in the course of engagement with what is being researched' (Gibbs, 2005). When I write about people in the circle, they must be able to see themselves in a way that respects their processes; but there are times when I feel it is more important to be inventive, to surprise, to suspend conventional thought.

A Glimpse of Inner Capacity

In exploring possible features of the trace archive, I hope that there have been glimpses and even 'vistas of inner capacity' that have been opened up, as Ndebele (1986: 157) wished for in his address on the rediscovery of the ordinary. Foregrounding ontology and affect, I have tried to create the feeling of jumping right in, suspending the conventions that overwhelm the writer and reader and teacher when learning about the writing of research. As a writing teacher, I know that it is vital that we help to uncover the hidden conventions of academic writing so that they can be shared and democratised. But this opening and exploration is not a one-way street that always heads towards a destination North and West, in English. There are several stories and reflections here about struggles with received frameworks that are presented as grids to be aligned with a universal view of 'reality'. We saw this in Thusi's resistance to received wisdom on how to understand inequality or climate change and her desire to work from a southern, postcolonial perspective, and in Kay's and Siwela's desire to explore the edges of their disciplines and make new connections. These glimpses gesture to where the previously silent and alienated writing subject has quickened, resisted, refused and yielded.

Affect has helped to hold the complicated politics of feeling that might enable us to explore the process of writing an extended research project. Staying with complex moments in the circle and beyond can suggest where there is room to manoeuvre that 'corresponds to how much of an experiential "depth" we can access towards a next step' (Massumi, 2015: xi). This space to manoeuvre can be glimpsed in struggles with facilitating the circle as in Chapter 1, where I try to describe the space of the circle and why it isn't a safe space in any uncomplicated way; in shared discussion on laughter in the group in Chapter 4, where laughter shakes the tree of language, and perhaps most strongly in the interviews with the three ex-circlers, Kay, Siwela and Tia. These interviews focus on the moments – the punctum – where the surface of the research process interview is pierced to suggest a suffusion of affect.

While the circle has been foregrounded in this study, it is not the only space where we can think of writing as thinking/learning. Ellsworth (2005: 122) writes about the smudge as coming with an 'openness to an elsewhere and an otherwise'. It is not just about accumulating knowledge, but about knowledge-making as an open process. All spaces are potentially open, it's about how we look at them. There are water points everywhere. Writing at the water point is an expression of learning as a smudge between a self and a self that knows more, and differently, to paraphrase Elsworth. This has the potential to prize open a vital space where what knowledge is considered Given and what might be New can be negotiated afresh.

Playing with Time

The circle offered experiences to counter the numbing and often humiliating effects of duration. Time, particularly Aeon or lived time, where the distinction between past and future is blurred, emerges as profoundly important. Chapter 5, 'One Word at a Time', explored this theme but it also appears as a challenge for research in Chapter 6, and re-emerges again in Chapter 7 where Aditi, Clement and I try to look back at the circle to describe its pedagogy. An aspect of circle practice that stays with participants is the way the bringing of two pages worked as a portal to the circle and to a wider experience of knowledge-making beyond the deadening effects of duration. The emerging author is in charge of what to bring, however significant the two pages feel at the time. They can bring something they feel proud of, or something they are struggling with, or something that might be interesting to the group. They are in charge of the clock. You don't have to bring anything until you feel ready. Both Kay and Clement experienced significant stretches where they froze and felt unable to write. But the circle kept them in touch with writing, enabling them to help others.

Some of the activities described here mess with time and invite disjuncture and confusion into the discussion about writing. The three circles activity normalises disjuncture and shaky alignment as students explore personal histories and unconscious processes, professional commitments and theoretical choices, often experienced as theoretical impositions. These spheres interact in ways that pull on different aspects of past, present and future.

Backgrounding measured time and the 'teleological temporalities' of the discipline that pre-exist with strong future orientations (Lapping, 2017) opens a window to affect and desire. We see this in Vuyo and Natasha's freewriting during the workshop on laughter. Vuyo's 'for a moment in time equality' and Natasha's 'sometimes doing academia is sore' express this.

Academic Literacies and Doctoral Writing as a Field of Inquiry

This book has tried to do something different in the belief that while it is important to understand how practices evolve and are mediated by power and privilege, we can get stuck in trying to search and name practices with accuracy and then to work backwards to pedagogy. While this work of identifying practices and genres is necessary, we have to recognise that it tends to be normative and to some extent closed. These genres and forms will become the things that we teach, that we assume will have magic powers to open doors, to career pathways and to 'new knowledge'. But literacy is also unbounded and fugitive, leaking and leaping in ways that don't want to be channeled. It wants to keep flowing. For teachers of writing this invites us to keep work and play close together, 'to keep the flow of difference, movement, sensation – and their destinations – open and undetermined' (Ellsworth, 2005: 175) as much as possible and desirable.

If we are to re-imagine the relationship between and knowledge-making beyond settled notions of literacy and social practices – ways of thinking, behaving, feeling and acting that come to be associated with certain realms of social life – we need to both situate more deeply and experiment more widely. As a contribution to situated knowledge, I have tried to write from where I am in the global south from uneven ground, to feel what it's like to write, to interrupt the strong narrative that the inevitable trajectory of text is towards the crusted epistemic centre.

The INK in ThINK

The phrase 'Put the INK in ThINK' was jotted down on one of the yellow folders that were the focus in Chapter 2. I liked the phrase but can't remember how I came across it. It expresses an important part of the method of this book, that the writing subject collides with all the different materialities while writing. The hands on the pen or the keyboard launch us forward, sideways and backwards in the moment as described in the freewriting in Chapter 4 on laughter. These faltering steps into uncertainty call language into question, making us encounter its slipperiness in the choice we have in what will stay on the page. This challenges the representational power that written language has, the myth that we can perfectly represent a research process, in this case an extended engagement with the writers' circle.

The phrase 'ink in think' is launched from an I. The realisation that pronouns are relational and an I is also always a we, and often a they, has been both sobering and empowering. It is empowering in that it has opened the possibility of seeing writing as ethical relationality: in Braidotti's words, 'Writing is living intensively and inhabiting language as a site of multiple others' (2014: 164). This means embracing ethics in a way that continues an open-ended discussion of possibilities. It is sobering to think this through. There is an understory of what emerged from following through with the dialogue of the ethics processes, new insights that emerged with Siwela, Ellen, Natasha, Vuyo, that I have only touched on here.

Divine discourse thrives on masking the I but it is important to take authorial responsibility. It is central to the project of this book to hover on the edge between subjective and objective and to make the interface visible. Because this is how we will begin to see the lineaments of the trace archive and to breathe life into the often-stuck groove of what is perceived to be Given and what might be New.

Writing and Knowledge-Making

My project has been to disrupt and re-size the status of the formal archive with its certainties and formulae that sometimes feel like magic tricks. I am not interested in replacing it. We don't need another hegemonic approach. It's about diffracting and interrupting to widen and deepen. Best to start with challenging the blindness of the hubris of the god view and divine discourse, and questioning the pervasiveness of the pipeline metaphor for bringing new voices and new knowledge in to the archive. Together, these contribute to the deficit discourse that creates a feeling of lack and of falling short pervading the research writing journey for postgraduate scholars. This reinforces the sense that the only task in the university is to chase an elusive imaginary of objective, placeless, universal and bloodless product – as many products as possible in the shortest possible time.

This book offers instead a reflectory of images, stories and theoretical resources over time to stretch and re-orient the formal archive that postgraduate scholars and their teachers shield and enact, to reconnect it to its experiential archive. This needs to be done again and again and again in different times and places.

The circle is like water. It smudges, flows, too much and not enough.
Like writing.

What if the water point dried up?

Would it leave a salty brine, like the rogue popcorn? Some smudges of
breath and ink in many languages? A new concept that made it to the
altar? A tender acknowledgement to front a thesis? A memory
of laughter?

There would be new water points, but we would have to know where to
look and how to listen.

References

Abdulatief, S. and Guzula, X. (2018) Emerging academics: Using WhatsApp to share novice and expert resources in a postgraduate writing group. In M.J. Curry and T. Lillis (eds) *Global Academic Publishing: Policies, Perspectives and Pedagogies* (pp. 249–263). Multilingual Matters.

Adam, B. (2004) *Time*. Polity Press.

Adorno, T. and Nicholsen, S. (1990) Punctuation marks. *The Antioch Review* 48 (3), 300–305.

Aitchison, C. and Guerin, C. (eds) (2014) *Writing Groups for Doctoral Education and Beyond: Innovations in Practice and Theory*. Routledge.

Antia, B. and Makoni, S. (eds) (2022) *Southernizing Sociolinguistics: Colonialism, Racism and Patriarchy in Language in the Global South*. Routledge.

Arao, B. and Clemens, K. (2013) From safe spaces to brave spaces: A new way to frame dialogue around diversity. In L.M. Landreman (ed.) *The Art of Effective Facilitation* (pp. 135–150). Stylus Publishing.

Arend, M. (2014) 'It was hardly about writing': Translations of experience on entering postgraduate studies. In L. Thesen and L. Cooper (eds) *Risk in Academic Writing: Postgraduates, Their Teachers and the Making of Knowledge* (pp. 219–233). Multilingual Matters.

Ashcroft, B. (2014) Knowing time: Temporal epistemology and the African novel. In B. Cooper and R. Morrell (eds) *Africa-Centred Knowledges: Crossing Fields & Worlds* (pp. 64–77). James Currey.

Badat, S. (2009) Theorising institutional change: Post-1994 South African higher education. *Studies in Higher Education* 34 (4), 455–467.

Badenhorst, C., Amell, B. and Burford, J. (eds) (2021) *Re-imagining Doctoral Writing*. The WAC Clearinghouse & University Press of Colorado.

Bakhtin, M.M. (1968) *Rabelais and His World* (trans. H. Iswolsky). M.I.T. Press.

Bakhtin, M.M. (1981) *The Dialogic Imagination: Four Essays* (trans. C. Emerson and M. Holquist). University of Texas Press.

Bakhtin, M.M (1986) *Speech Genres and Other Late Essays* (trans. V.W. McGee). University of Texas Press.

Ball, A., Makoni, S., Smitherman, G. and Spears, A.K. (eds) (2003) *Black Linguistics: Language, Society and Politics in Africa and the Americas*. Routledge.

Ball, S.J. (2012/2021) The making of a neoliberal academic. *Research in Teacher Education* 11 (1), 15–17.

Ballard, B. and Clanchy, J. (1988) Literacy in the university: An anthropological approach. In G.B. Taylor, B. Beasley, H. Bock, J. Clancy and P. Nightingale (eds) *Literacy by Degrees* (pp. 7–23). SRHE/The Open University.

Bangeni, B. and Kapp, R. (2005) Identities in transition: Shifting conceptions of Home among 'Black' South African university students. *African Studies Review* 48 (3), 1–19.

Bangeni, B. and Kapp, R. (eds) (2017) *Negotiating Learning and Identity in Higher Education: Access, Persistence and Retention*. Bloomsbury Publishing.

Bangeni, B. and Pym, J. (2017) The role of religion in mediating the transition to higher education. In B. Bangeni and J. Pym (eds) *Negotiating Learning and Identity in Higher Education: Access, Persistence and Retention* (pp. 95–108). Continuum.

Barad, K. (2012) On touching: The inhuman that therefore I am. *Differences* 23 (3), 206–223.

Barnard, I. (2014) *Upsetting Composition Commonplaces*. University Press of Colorado.

Barthes, R. (1981) *Camera Lucida: Reflections on Photography* (trans. R. Howard). Hill and Wang.

Benjamin, W. (1999) *The Arcades Project* (trans. H. Eiland and K. McLaughlin). The Belknap Press of Harvard University.

Berger, J. (2011) *Bento's Sketchbook*. Verso.

Bergson, H. (1914) *Laughter: An Essay on the Meaning of the Comic* (trans. C. Brereton and F. Rothwell). Macmillan.

Bhabha, H.K. (1994) *The Location of Culture*. Routledge.

Biggs, J. and Tang, C. (2007) *Using Constructive Alignment in Outcomes-Based Teaching and Learning Teaching for Quality Learning at University*. Open University Press.

Biko, S. (1978) *I Write what I Like*. Bowerdean Press.

Billig, M. (2005) *Laughter and Ridicule: Towards A Social Critique of Humour*. SAGE Publications.

Billig, M. (2008) The language of critical discourse analysis: The case of nominalization. *Discourse & Society* 19 (6), 783–800.

Blackawton, P.S., Airzee, S., Allen, A., Baker, S., Berrow, A., Blair, C., Churchill, M., Coles, J., Cumming, R.F.J., Fraquelli, L., Hackford, C., Hinton Mellor, A., Hutchcroft, M., Ireland, B., Jewsbury, D., Littlejohns, A., Littlejohns, G.M., Lotto, M., McKeown, J., O'Toole, A., Richards, H., Robbins-Davey, L., Roblyn, S., Rodwell-Lynn, H., Schenck, D., Springer, J., Wishy, A., Rodwell-Lynn, T., Strudwick, D. and Lotto, R.B. (2011) Blackawton bees. *Biology Letters* 7 (2), 168–172.

Blommaert, J. (2005) *Discourse*. Cambridge University Press.

Boldt, G. and Leander, K.M. (2020) Affect theory in reading research: Imagining the radical difference. *Reading Psychology* 41 (6), 515–532.

Bosanquet, A., Cahir, J. and Huber, E. (2014) An intimate circle: Reflections on writing as women in higher education. In C. Aitchison and C. Guerin (eds) *Writing Groups for Doctoral Education and Beyond* (pp. 220–233). Routledge.

Boughey, C. and McKenna, S. (2016) Academic literacy and the decontextualised learner. *Critical Studies in Teaching and Learning (CriSTaL)* 4 (2), 1–9.

Bourdieu, P., Passeron, J.-C. and de Saint-Martin, M. (1994) *Academic Discourse: Linguistic Misunderstanding and Professorial Power* (trans. R. Teese). Stanford University Press.

Bowker, G.C. (2005) *Memory Practices in the Sciences*. MIT Press.

Bowker, G.C. (2010) The archive. *Communication and Critical/Cultural Studies* 7 (2), 212–214.

Braidotti, R. (2014) Writing as a nomadic subject. *Comparative Critical Studies* 11 (2–3), 163–184.

Butler J. (1990) *Gender Trouble: Feminism and the Subversion of Identity*. Routledge.

Butler, J. (1993) *Bodies that Matter: On the Discursive Limits of 'Sex'*. Routledge.

Cadman, K. (2003) Divine discourse: Plagiarism, hybridity and epistemological racism. In S. May, M. Franken and R. Barnard (eds) *LED 2003, 1st International Conference on Language, Education & Diversity. Refereed Proceedings and Keynotes*. University of Waikato.

Cadman, K. (2014) Of house and home: Reflections on knowing and writing for a 'Southern' postgraduate pedagogy. In L. Thesen and L. Cooper (eds) *Risk in Academic Writing: Postgraduates, Their Teachers and the Making of Knowledge* (pp. 166–200). Multilingual Matters.

Canagarajah, S. and Lee, E. (2014) Negotiating alternative discourses in academic writing and publishing: Risks with hybridity. In L. Thesen and L. Cooper (eds) *Risk in Academic Writing: Postgraduate Students, Their Teachers and the Making of Knowledge* (pp. 59–99). Multilingual Matters.

Casanave, C.P. (2010) Taking risks?: A case study of three doctoral students writing qualitative dissertations at an American university in Japan. *Journal of Second Language Writing* 19 (1), 1–16.

Casanave, C.P. and Vandrick, S. (2003) *Writing for Scholarly Publication: Behind the Scenes in Language Education*. Lawrence Erlbaum Associates.

Castro-Gomez, S. (2021) *Zero Point Hubris: Science, Race and Enlightenment in Eighteenth-century Latin America* (trans. G. Ciccariello-Maher and D.T. Deere). Rowman and Littlefield.

Chihota, M.C. (2007) 'The games people play': Taking on postgraduate identities in the context of writer circles. *Journal of Applied Linguistics* 4 (1), 131–136.

Chihota, C. M. and Thesen, L. (2014) Rehearsing 'the postgraduate condition' in writers' circles. In L. Thesen and L. Cooper (eds) *Risk in Academic Writing: Postgraduate Students, Their Teachers and the Making of Knowledge* (pp. 131–147). Multilingual Matters.

Choi, S., Selmeczi, A. and Strausz, E. (eds) (2020) *Critical Methods for the Study of World Politics: Creativity and Transformation*. Routledge.

Clark, R. and Ivanic, R. (1997) *The Politics of Writing*. Routledge.

Cloete, N. and Mouton, J. (2015) *Doctoral Education in South Africa*. African Minds.

Clough, P. and Halley, J. (2007) *The Affective Turn: Theorizing the Social*. Duke University Press.

Coleman, L. (ed.) (2018) *Teaching in Extended Programmes in South Africa: Classroom Contexts, Lecturer Identities and Teaching Practices*. Centre for Higher Education, Cape Peninsula University of Technology.

Coleman, L. and Thesen, L. (2018) Theory as a verb: Working with dilemmas in educational development. *SOTL in the South* 2 (1), 129–135.

Coleman, R. and Ringrose, J. (eds) (2013) *Deleuze and Research Methodologies*. Edinburgh University Press.

Collyer, F. and Dufoix, S. (2022) Rethinking the epistemic compass. *Revue d'histoire Des Sciences Humaines* 41.

Comaroff, J. and Comaroff, J.L. (2012) *Theory from the South: Or, How Euro-America is Evolving toward Africa*. Paradigm Publishers.

Connell, R. (2007) *Southern Theory: The Global Dynamics of Knowledge in Social Science*. Polity.

Cooper, D. (2015) Social justice and South African university student enrolment data by 'race', 1998–2012: From 'skewed revolution' to 'stalled revolution'. *Higher Education Quarterly* 69 (3), 237–262.

Cooper, L. (2014) 'Does my experience count?' The role of experiential knowledge in the research writing of postgraduate adult learners. In L. Thesen and L. Cooper (eds) *Risk in Academic Writing: Postgraduate Students, Their Teachers and the Making of Knowledge* (pp. 27–47). Multilingual Matters.

Costandius, E. (2019) Fostering the conditions for creative concept development. *Cogent Education* 6 (1).

Council of Higher Education (2000) *Towards A New Higher Education Landscape: Meeting The Equity, Quality and Social Development Imperatives of South Africa in the 21st Century*. Pretoria.

Cusk, R. (2014) *Outline*. Vintage.

Darwin, C. (2009) *The Annotated Origin: A Facsimile of the First Edition of On the Origin of Species* (annotation J.T. Costa). The Belknap Press of Harvard University Press.

Deleuze, G. (2004) *The Logic of Sense*. Continuum.

Deleuze, G. and Guattari, F. (1987) *A Thousand Plateaus: Capitalism and Schizophrenia* (trans. B. Massumi). University of Minnesota Press.

Derrida, J. (1976) *Of Grammatology.* Johns Hopkins University Press.

Derrida, J. (1996) *Archive Fever: A Freudian Impression* (trans. E. Prenowitz). The University of Chicago Press.

Deyi, S. (2014) A lovely imposition: The complexity of writing a thesis in isiXhosa. In L. Thesen and L. Cooper (eds) *Risk in Academic Writing: Postgraduate Students, Their Teachers and the Making of Knowledge* (pp. 48–56). Multilingual Matters.

Dlamini, J. (2009) *Native Nostalgia.* Jacana Media.

Dyer, G. (1998) *Out of Sheer Rage: In the Shadow of D.H. Lawrence.* Abacus.

Eagleton, T. (1990) *The Significance of Theory.* Wiley-Blackwell.

Elbow, P. (1991) Reflections on academic discourse: How it relates to freshman and colleagues. *College English* 53 (2), 135.

Elbow, P. (1998) *Writing Without Teachers.* Oxford University Press.

Ellsworth, E.A. (2005) *Places of Learning: Media, Architecture, Pedagogy.* Routledge.

Entwistle, N.J. and Ramsden, P. (1983) *Understanding Student Learning.* Nichols Pub. Co.

Ferrante, E. (2014) *Those Who Leave and Those Who Stay: The Neapolitan Novels, Book Three* (trans. A. Goldstein). Europa Editions.

Firbas, J. (1971) *On the Concept of Communicative Dynamism in the Theory of Functional Sentence Perspective.* Universitas Brunensis, Facultas Philosophae, Studia Menora. Online at digilib2.phil.muni.cz.

Foucault, M. (1977) *Discipline and Punish: The Birth of the Prison* (trans. A. Sheridan). Vintage Books.

Foucault, M. (1998) Different spaces. In M. Foucault (ed., trans. R. Hurley) *Essential Works of Foucault 1954–1984* (vol. 2, pp. 175–185). Penguin.

Frick, L., McKenna, S. and Muthama, E. (2017) Death of the PhD: When industry partners determine doctoral outcomes. *Higher Education Research and Development* 36 (2), 444–447.

Fried, M. (2005) Barthes's punctum. *Critical Inquiry* 31 (3), 539–574.

Gee, J.P. (1990) *Social Linguistics and Literacies: Ideology in Discourses.* Falmer.

Gibbs, A. (2005) Fictocriticism, affect, mimesis: Engendering differences. *TEXT* 9 (1).

Gibbs, A. (2015) Writing as method: Attunement, resonance, and rhythm. In B. Timm Knudsen and C. Stage (eds) *Affective Methodologies: Developing Cultural Research Strategies for the Study of Affect* (pp. 222–236). Palgrave Macmillan.

Gillespie, K. and Naidoo, L.-A. (2019) Introduction. *The South Atlantic Quarterly* 118 (1), 190–194.

Goffman, E. (1967) *Interaction Ritual: Essays on Face-to-Face Behavior.* Anchor Books.

Goffman, E. (1981) *Forms of Talk.* University of Pennsylvania Press.

Grant, B. and Knowles, S. (2000) Flights of imagination: Academic women be(com)ing writers. *International Journal for Academic Development* 5 (1), 6–19.

Gregg, M. and Seigworth, G. (eds) (2010) *The Affect Theory Reader.* Duke University Press.

Halliday, M.A.K. (1985) *An Introduction to Functional Grammar.* Edward Arnold.

Hanley, C. (2019) Thinking with Deleuze and Guattari: An exploration of writing as assemblage. *Educational Philosophy and Theory* 51 (4), 413–423.

Haraway, D. (1988) Situated knowledges: The science question in feminism and the privilege of partial perspective. *Feminist Studies* 14 (3), 575–599.

Haraway, D. (2004) *The Haraway Reader.* Routledge.

Haraway, D.J. (2016) *Staying with the Trouble: Making Kin in the Chthulucene.* Duke University Press.

Herman, C. (2011) Expanding doctoral education in South Africa: Pipeline or pipedream? *Higher Education Research and Development* 30 (4), 505–517.

Herring, E. (2020) *Laughter is Vital.* Aeon.

Herrington, A. and Curtis, M.S. (2000) *Persons in Process: Four Stories of Writing and Personal Development in College*. National Council of Teachers of English.

Hirson, D. (2004) *I remember King Kong (the boxer)*. Jacana.

Hofmeyr, I. (2006) Reflections on Achille Mbembe's 'On the Postcolony': Achille Mbembe in conversation with Isabel Hofmeyr. *South African Historical Journal* 56 (1), 177–187.

hooks, b. (1991) Theory as liberatory practice. *Yale Journal of Law and Feminism* 4 (1), 1.

Howie, P. and Bagnall, R. (2013) A critique of the deep and surface approaches to learning model. *Teaching in Higher Education* 18 (4), 389–400.

Ingold, T. (2007) *Lines: A Brief History*. Routledge.

Ivanič, R. (1998) *Writing and Identity: The Discoursal Construction of Identity in Academic Writing*. John Benjamins.

Ivanič, R. and Camps, D. (2001) I am how I sound: Voice as self-representation in L2 writing. *Journal of Second Language Writing* 10 (1–2), 3–33.

Jackson, A.Y. and Mazzei, L.A. (2013) Plugging one text into another: Thinking with theory in qualitative research. *Qualitative Inquiry* 19 (4), 261–271.

Jacobs, C. (2005) On being an insider on the outside: New spaces for integrating academic literacies. *Teaching in Higher Education* 10 (4), 475–487.

Jansen, J. (2003) The state of higher education in South Africa: From massification to mergers. *State of the Nation: South Africa* 2004, 290–311.

Jansen, J.D. (2009) *Knowledge in the Blood: Confronting Race and the Apartheid Past*. Stanford University Press.

Janz, B.B. (2001) The territory is not the map: Place, Deleuze and Guattari, and African philosophy. *Philosophy Today* 45 (4), 392–405.

Kamler, B. and Thomson, P. (2006) *Helping Doctoral Students Write: Pedagogies for Supervision*. Routledge.

Khanyile, B. (2021) Violences in the South African student movement. In S.C. Swartz, A. Cooper, C.M. Batan and L. Kropff-Causa (eds) *Oxford Handbook of Global South Youth Studies* (pp. 185–200). Oxford University Press.

King, S. (2000) *On Writing: A Memoir of the Craft*. Simon and Schuster.

King, S. (2008) *The Stand*. Anchor.

Knudsen, B.T. and Stage, C. (eds) (2015) *Affective Methodologies: Developing Cultural Research Strategies for the Study of Affect*. Palgrave Macmillan.

Kraftl, P. (2016) Emotional geographies and the study of education spaces. In M. Zembylas and P. Schutz (eds) *Methodological Advances in Research on Emotion and Education* (pp. 151–163). Springer.

Lakoff, G. and Johnson, M. (1980) *Metaphors We Live By*. University of Chicago Press.

Lapping, C. (2017) The explosion of real time and the structural conditions of temporality in a society of control: Durations and urgencies of academic research. *Discourse: Studies in the Cultural Politics of Education* 38 (6), 906–922.

Law, J. and Urry, J. (2004) Enacting the social. *Economy and Society* 33 (3), 390–410.

Lea, M.R. and. Street, B.V. (1998) Student writing in higher education: An academic literacies approach. *Studies in Higher Education* 23 (2), 157–172.

Leander, K. and Boldt, G. (2013) Rereading 'A pedagogy of multiliteracies': Bodies, texts, and emergence. *Journal of Literacy Research* 45 (1), 22–46.

Liardét, C.L. (2015) Academic literacy and grammatical metaphor: Mapping development. *TESOL International Journal* 10 (1), 29–46.

Lillis, T. (2008) Ethnography as method, methodology, and 'deep theorizing': Closing the gap between text and context in academic writing research. *Written Communication* 25 (3), 353–388.

Lillis, T. (2017) Resistir regimenes de evaluacion en el estudio del escribir: Hacia un imaginario enriquecido. *Signo y pensamiento* 36 (71), 66–81.

Lillis, T. and Scott, M. (2007) Defining academic literacies research: Issues of epistemology, ideology and strategy. *Journal of Applied Linguistics and Professional Practice* 4 (1), 5–32.

Lillis, T.M. and Curry, M.J. (2010) *Academic Writing in a Global Context: The Politics and Practices of Publishing in English*. Routledge.

Lillis, T. and Maybin, J. (2017) Introduction: The dynamics of textual trajectories in professional and workplace practice. *Text & Talk* 37 (4), 409–414.

Lillis, T., Harrington, K., Lea, M.R. and Mitchell, S. (2015) *Working with Academic Literacies: Case Studies Towards Transformative Practice*. The WAC Clearinghouse and Parlor Press.

Lombard, E. (2016) The work of nostalgia in Denis Hirson's 'I Remember King Kong (The Boxer)'. *English in Africa* 43 (3), 19–41.

Long, W. (2021) *Nation on the Couch: Inside South Africa's Mind*. Melinda Ferguson Books.

Lord, B. (2006) Foucault's museum: Difference, representation, and genealogy. *Museum and Society* 4 (1), 1–14.

Lury, C. and Wakeford, N. (eds) (2012) *Inventive Methods: The Happening of the Social*. Routledge.

Lykke, N.B., Brewster, A., Davis, K., Koobak, R., Lei, S. and Peto, A. (eds) (2014) *Writing Academic Texts Differently: Intersectional Feminist Methodologies and the Playful Art of Writing*. Routledge.

Lyng, S. (1990) Edgework: A social psychological analysis of voluntary risk taking. *The American Journal of Sociology* 95 (4), 851–886.

Maart, R. (2014) Exordium: Writing and the relation: From textual coloniality to South African Black consciousness. In M. Michlin and J.-P. Rocchi (eds) *Black Intersectionalities: A Critique for the 21st Century*. Liverpool University Press.

MacLure, M. (2013) The wonder of data. *Cultural Studies, Critical Methodologies* 13 (4), 228–232.

Maldonado-Torres, N. (2007) On the coloniality of being: Contributions to the development of a concept. *Cultural Studies* 21 (2–3), 240–270.

Manathunga, C. (2019) 'Timescapes' in doctoral education: The politics of temporal equity in higher education. *Higher Education Research and Development* 38 (6), 1227–1239.

Martin, J.R. (2008) Incongruent and proud: De-vilifying 'nominalization'. *Discourse & Society* 19 (6), 801–810.

Marton, F. and Saljo. R. (1976) On qualitative differences in learning 1 – Outcomes and process. *The British Journal of Educational Psychology* 46 (1), 4–11.

Massumi, B. (1987) Translator's foreword: Pleasures of philosophy. In G. Deleuze and F. Guattari (eds) *A Thousand Plateaus: Capitalism and Schizophrenia* (pp. ix–xiv). University of Minnesota Press.

Massumi, B. (2002) *Parables for The Virtual: Movement, Affect, Sensation*. Duke University Press.

Massumi, B. (2015) *Politics of Affect*. Polity.

Mbembe, A. (2001) *On the Postcolony*. University of California Press.

Mbembe, A. (2002) The power of the archive and its limits. In V. Harris, C. Hamilton, J. Taylor, M. Pickover, G. Reid and R. Saleh (eds) *Refiguring the Archive* (pp. 19–26). David Philip Publishers, Kluwer.

Mbembe, A. (2016) Decolonizing the university: New directions. *Arts and Humanities in Higher Education* 15 (1), 29–45.

McConlogue, T., Mitchell, S. and Peake, K. (2012) Thinking writing at Queen Mary, University of London. In C. Thaiss, G. Bräuer, P. Carlino and L. Ganobcsik-Williams (eds) *Writing Programs Worldwide: Profiles of Academic Writing in Many Places* (pp. 203–211). The WAC Clearinghouse and Parlor Press.

McKinney, C. (2017) *Language and Power in Post-colonial Schooling: Ideologies in Practice*. Routledge.

McKinney, C. and Christie, P. (eds) (2022) *Decoloniality, Language and Literacy: Conversations with Teacher Educators*. Multilingual Matters.

Mkula, L. (2018) Language ideologies and decoloniality in Vernac News. PhD thesis. University of Cape Town. http://hdl.handle.net/11427/29426

Nagar, R. (2019) *Hungry Translations*: Relearning the World through Radical Vulnerability. In journeys with Sangtin Kisan Mazdoor Sangathan and Parakh Theatre. University of Illinois Press.

Nagar, R. and Selmeczi, A. (2019) The labour of political theatre as embodied politics: A conversation. In S. Choi, A. Selmeczi and E. Strausz (eds) *Critical Methods for the Study of World Politics* (pp. 84–101). Routledge.

Nagar, R. and Shirazi, R. (2019) Radical vulnerability. *Keywords in Radical Geography, Antipode at 50*, 236–242.

Nagar, R., Meier, I. and Spathopoulou, A. (2023) Refusals, radical vulnerability, and hungry translations – A conversation with Richa Nagar. *Fennia-International Journal of Geography*.

Ndebele, N.S. (1986) The rediscovery of the ordinary: Some new writings in South Africa. *Journal of Southern African Studies* 12 (2), 143–157.

Ndlovu-Gatsheni, S.J. (2015) Decoloniality as the future of Africa: Decoloniality, Africa, power, knowledge, being. *History Compass* 13 (10), 485–496.

Newfield, D. (2014) Transformation, transduction and the transmodal moment. In C. Jewitt (ed.) *The Routledge Handbook of Multimodal Analysis* (pp. 100–113). Routledge.

Ngũgĩ wa Thiongo (1986) *Decolonising The Mind: The Politics of Language in African Literature*. John Currey.

Nieuwenhuis, M. (2019) Ephemeral language: Communicating by breath. In S. Choi, A. Selmeczi and E. Strausz (eds) *Critical Methods for the Study of World Politics* (pp. 39–62). Routledge.

Nyamnjoh, F.B. (2016) *#RhodesMustFall: Nibbling at Resilient Colonialism in South Africa*. Langaa Research and Publishing Common Initiative Group.

Paxton, M. (2014) Genre: A pigeonhole or a pigeon? Case studies of the dilemmas posed by the writing of academic research proposals. In L. Thesen and L. Cooper (eds) *Risk in Academic Writing: Postgraduate Students, Their Teachers and the Making of Knowledge* (pp. 148–165). Multilingual Matters.

Pennycook, A. (2018) Applied linguistics as epistemic assemblage. *AILA Review* 31 (1), 113–134.

Pennycook, A. and Makoni, S. (2020) *Innovations and Challenges in Applied Linguistics from the Global South*. Routledge.

Peseta, T., Barrie, S. and McLean, J. (2017) Academic life in the measured university: Pleasures, paradoxes and politics. *Higher Education Research and Development* 36 (3), 453–457.

Pillow, W. (2003) Confession, catharsis, or cure? Rethinking the uses of reflexivity as methodological power in qualitative research. *International Journal of Qualitative Studies in Education* 16 (2), 175–196.

Pratt, M.L. (1991) Arts of the contact zone. *Profession*, 33–40.

Prinsloo, M. (2022) Moving dirt: Relationality and complementarity of domestic workers. *Journal of Postcolonial Linguistics* 7, 89–107.

Prinsloo, M. and Breier, M. (1996) *The Social Uses of Literacy: Theory and Practice in Contemporary South Africa*. John Benjamins Publishing.

Probyn, E. (2005) *Blush: Faces of Shame*. University of Minnesota Press.

Probyn, E., Bozalek, V., Shefer, T. and Carolissen, R. (2019) Productive faces of shame: An interview with Elspeth Probyn. *Feminism & Psychology* 29 (2), 322–334.

Reddy, M. (1979) The conduit metaphor. *Metaphor and Thought* 2, 285–324.

Reynolds, J. (2007) Wounds and scars: Deleuze on the time and ethics of the event. *Deleuze Studies* 1 (2), 144–166.

Rovelli, C. (2018) *The Order of Time* (trans. E. Segre and S. Carnell). Allen Lane.

Rudwick, S. and Makoni, S. (2021) Southernizing and decolonizing the sociology of language: African scholarship matters. *International Journal of the Sociology of Language* 267–268, 259–263.

Said, E.W. (1979) *Orientalism*. Vintage Books.

Samson, S., Hutchings, C., Goolam Hoosen, T. and Thesen, L. (2021) 'I am everywhere all at once': Pipelines, rhizomes and research writing. *Higher Education* 83 (6), 1207–1223.

Schroeder, C.L., Fox, H. and Bizzell, P. (2002) *ALT DIS: Alternative Discourses and the Academy*. Boynton/Cook Heinemann.

Shepherd, L.J. (1993) *Lifting the Veil: The Feminine Face of Science*. Shambhala Publications.

Shouse, E. (2005) Feeling, emotion, affect. *M/c journal* 8 (6).

Simba, P. (2021) A feminist critique of ubuntu: Implications for citizenship education in Zimbabwe. PhD thesis, Stellenbosch University.

Smith, D.W. (2012) *Essays on Deleuze*. Edinburgh University Press.

St Pierre, E.A. (2018) Writing post qualitative inquiry. *Qualitative Inquiry* 24 (9), 603–608.

St Pierre, E.A. (2019) Post qualitative inquiry in an ontology of immanence. *Qualitative Inquiry* 25 (1), 3–16.

St Pierre, E. (2021) Post qualitative inquiry, the refusal of method, and the risk of the new. *Qualitative Inquiry* 27 (1), 3–9.

Stagoll, C. (2005) Event. In A. Parr (ed.) *The Deleuze Dictionary* (pp. 87–89). Edinburgh University Press.

Starke-Meyerring, D. (2014) Writing groups as critical spaces for engaging normalized institutional cultures of writing in doctoral education. In C. Aitchison and C. Guerin (eds) *Writing Groups for Doctoral Education and Beyond* (pp. 65–81). Routledge.

Staunton, I. (2005) *Writing Now: More Stories from Zimbabwe*. Weaver Press.

Steyn, M. (2012) The ignorance contract: Recollections of apartheid childhoods and the construction of epistemologies of ignorance. *Identities* 19 (1), 8–25.

Street, B.V. (1984) *Literacy in Theory and Practice*. Cambridge University Press.

Street, B.V. (1993) Culture is a verb: Anthropological aspects of language and cultural process. In D. Graddol, L. Thompson and M. Byram (eds) *Language and Culture* (Chapter 2). Multilingual Matters.

Swales, J.M. (2004) *Research Genres: Explorations and Applications*. Cambridge University Press.

Swales, J. and Feak, C. (2009) *Abstracts and the Writing of Abstracts*. University of Michigan Press.

Taussig, M. (2015) *The Corn Wolf*. University of Chicago Press.

Thesen, L. (2013) Risk in postgraduate writing: Voice, discourse and edgework. *Critical Studies in Teaching and Learning* 1 (1), 123–136.

Thesen, L. (2014) 'If they're not laughing, watch out!': Emotion and risk in postgraduate writers' circles. In C. Aichison and C. Guerin (eds) *Writing Groups for Doctoral Education and Beyond* (pp. 162–176). Routledge.

Thesen, L. and van Pletzen, E. (eds) (2006) *Academic Literacy and the Languages of Change*. Continuum.

Thesen, L. and Cooper, L. (eds) (2014) *Risk in Academic Writing: Postgraduate Students, Their Teachers and the Making of Knowledge*. Multilingual Matters.

Tronto, J. (1993) *Moral Boundaries: A Political Argument for An Ethic of Care*. Routledge.

Tuck, J. (2016) 'That ain't going to get you a professorship': Discourses of writing and the positioning of academics' work with student writers in UK higher education. *Studies in Higher Education* 41 (9), 1612–1626.

Turner, J. (2018) *On Writtenness: The Cultural Politics of Academic Writing*. Bloomsbury Academic.

Verran, H. (1999) Staying true to the laughter in Nigerian classrooms. *The Sociological Review* 47 (1), 136–155.

Verran, H. (2007) Metaphysics and learning. *Learning Inquiry* 1 (1), 31–39.

Wakeling, P. and Kyriakou, C. (2010) *Widening Participation from Undergraduate to Postgraduate Degrees: A Research Synthesis*. The University of York.

Waterton, C. (2007) Taking a non-linear plunge into the mnemonick deep. *Metascience* 16 (2), 179–203.

Waugh, C. (2019) In defence of safe spaces: Subaltern counterpublics and vulnerable politics in the neoliberal university. In M. Breeze, Y. Taylor and C. Costa (eds) *Time and Space in the Neoliberal University: Futures and Fractures in Higher Education* (pp. 143–168). Palgrave Macmillan.

Willett, C. (2014) *Interspecies Ethics*. Columbia University Press.

Winnicott, D.W. (1989) *Playing and Reality*. Routledge.

Zembylas, M., Bozalek, V. and Shefer, T. (2014) Tronto's notion of privileged irresponsibility and the reconceptualisation of care: Implications for critical pedagogies of emotion in higher education. *Gender and Education* 26 (3), 200–214.

Index

For Product Safety Concerns and Information please contact our EU Authorised Representative:

Easy Access System Europe

Mustamäe tee 50

10621 Tallinn

Estonia

gpsr.requests@easproject.com

www.ingramcontent.com/pod-product-compliance
Lightning Source LLC
Chambersburg PA
CBHW062036270326
41929CB00014B/2442